Instructor's Manual to Accompany Dominick

THE DYNAMICS OF MASS COMMUNICATION

FIFTH EDITION

JERRY PINKHAM

College of Lake County

The McGraw-Hill Companies, Inc.

New York St. Louis San Francisco Auckland Bogotá
Caracas Lisbon London Madrid Mexico City Milan Montreal
New Delhi San Juan Singapore Sydney Tokyo Toronto

McGraw-Hill

A Division of The McGraw·Hill Companies

Instructor's Manual to Accompany Dominick
THE DYNAMICS OF MASS COMMUNICATION
Fifth Edition

Copyright © 1996 by The McGraw-Hill Companies Inc. All rights reserved.
Printed in the United States of America. The contents, or
parts thereof, may be reproduced for use with
THE DYNAMICS OF MASS COMMUNICATION
Fifth Edition
by Joseph R. Dominick
provided such reproductions bear copyright notice, but may not
be reproduced in any form for any other purpose without
permission of the publisher.

ISBN 0-07-017997-2

234567890 GDP GDP 90987

TABLE OF CONTENTS

Chapter

INTRODUCTION

This manual is designed for both you *and* your students. For the instructor, it offers over 800 test questions. Each chapter comes with 15 true/false questions and 20 multiple-choice items. Then in *Appendix B* you'll find a unique and comprehensive final exam which you can easily adapt to your particular course needs and approach.

For students, each chapter comes offers a one-page study guide and the "Topics for Discussion" sheet. You can easily transform the latter (over 275 items total) into class projects, essay questions, homework assignments, or term-paper topics.

Each chapter is arranged the same. The first two pages serve as a class handout. Page one has three elements that should answer your students' most common questions:

SUMMARY: What's this chapter about? (without giving them enough details to skip the text)

CHAPTER OBJECTIVES: What general knowledge and insights do you expect me to understand from this chapter?

KEY TERMS AND CONCEPTS: What ideas should I study or, "What's going to be on the test?" Incidently, tests correspond *directly* with these keys words and concepts. I've also added checkoff boxes "[ ]" so that you can include or exclude any terms in any combination you choose; students should also find the boxes useful for checking off items as they learn them.

Page two offers what I hope are realistic, challenging, and up-to-date ideas for class discussions or projects. The purpose of the questions, of course, is to get students to think about what they've read in the text. Here they'll get a chance to reexamine their own beliefs and values and to explore current media issues as they affect both society and their own lives.

The true/false tests have fifteen questions each. These tests are printed on one page so that you can easily photocopy them. Use these questions as a stand-alone chapter test or with the multiple-choice items for a comprehensive unit exam. Most of the T/F questions parallel, but don't repeat, the multiple-choice points so that you won't risk asking the same question twice.

Like the T/F questions, many of the multiple-choice items are designed to test the students' ability to actually *apply* mass media concepts, not simply to test their capacity to memorize a text.

I've also tried to tackle the "but-why-isn't-this-answer-correct-also?" problem. It's inevitable in some test questions (certainly in an 800+ test bank) that some people will view a question differently than intended. Their viewpoint may lead to a different conclusion than the instructor's. Sometimes a different spin on a response is just as intellectually valid as the original conclusion. The "Test Appeal Procedure" in *Appendix A* addresses this problem. It provides an easy yet effective way by which students can challenge an answer. This process should be individual and private to preclude the "herd instinct" in class (you're familiar with that, the one where fifteen other students raise their hands and say, "Hey, that's what I was thinking too!" Right). This way you give credit where credit is due.

Appendix B is a final exam idea that was inspired by E. D. Hirsch, Jr's. book, *Cultural Literacy*. His thesis is that there is a certain body of terms and concepts that an educated citizenship must know in order to intelligently communicate with one another. On a smaller but parallel scale, I've modified that idea for a mass media final exam, i.e. there is a core body of ideas that communication students need to know in order to discuss the media in an informed way.

Hirsch (and a few hundred others) came up with about 2500 terms. In contrast, my list is self-selected, shorter, and confined to terms you'll find in *The Dynamics of Mass Communication*. As such, this list is obviously intended as a starting point for customizing your own list. In many ways, it's the list itself--not the exam--that's most significant. It says to your students, "These terms and concepts are the core knowledge I want you to know--these ideas (and your ability to apply them) are the reason for this course." By the way, the list also serves a by-product function by reducing their inevitable anxiety about what the final exam will be like and what it will cover.

I hope you'll find this manual accomplishes what it set out to do: make your job as a teacher just a little bit easier.

And last, a special thanks to Joseph R. Dominick for making this latest edition of *The Dynamics of Mass Communication* as information rich, anecdotally interesting, and intellectually rewarding as all the books he's somehow managed to find time to write.

Jerry W. Pinkham

P.S. For a computer software version of all the test questions, see your local McGraw-Hill book representative, or call 1-800-338-3987.

Chapter 1

The Nature and Function of Mass Communication Systems

This chapter explores the basic operational principles behind the communication process and the components that make that process work. We'll see how people communicate from an interpersonal setting to a mass media level, and why various types of "noise" can impede, alter, or even totally change the messages we send one another. We end by surveying the increasingly complex, fragile, and fractionalized nature of mass media, examining why it's happening and what it means to you, our society, and the world at large.

CHAPTER OBJECTIVES

. learn how communication works as a process and how the inherent elements interrelate

. see how "noise" interferes with communication process (from simple annoyance to total misunderstanding)

. investigate the differences between machine-assisted communication and that which isn't

. consider why the media targets their messages to increasingly more discreet audiences

KEY TERMS AND CONCEPTS

[ ] communication process and elements:
    [ ] source; [ ] encoding; [ ] message; [ ] channels; [ ] decoding; [ ] receiver;
    [ ] feedback (positive v negative; immediate v delayed)
[ ] noise (semantic - mechanical - environmental); [ ] message fidelity
[ ] interpersonal communication (simple and machine-assisted)
[ ] mass communications
    [ ] audience characteristics: large, heterogeneous, geographically diverse; self-selected
    [ ] mass communication source characteristics: produced by complex, formal organizations; have
        multiple gatekeepers; expensive to operate; exist to make a profit; highly competitive
[ ] conceptual models help us *organize*, *explain*, and *predict* complex relationships
[ ] media fractionalization (or segmentation)
[ ] symbiotic media relationships
[ ] convergence: distribution; content; hardware

TOPICS FOR DISCUSSION

1. Identify three distinct examples of interpersonal communication, machine-assisted interpersonal communication and mass communication that you experienced before coming to class today.

2. After the 1992 Los Angeles riots several black citizens complained that neighborhood Korean-American store owners often seemed rude, e.g., they rarely smiled. In response, the Korean-Americans said that people who smiled in public in *their* culture were perceived as "airheads." This shows how dangerous "semantic noise" can sometimes be. Yet cultural differences like this abound in the U.S. Cite parallel examples of cultural misunderstandings caused by semantic noise in other communication settings.

3. Can you act as your own personal "gatekeeper?" Are the results generally restrictive or nonrestrictive in terms of the knowledge and experiences you select to receive?

4. Describe how body language is used as a channel for feedback. In what ways do you see it used in the media? Does semantic noise ever play a role in body language?

5. Identify how cable networks personify media fractionalization.

6. What effects (good and bad) might this type of self-selected media specialization have on society and individuals?

7. Cite some examples of media convergence that you now presently enjoy that weren't even around when you began high school.

8. Volunteer a personal-experience example of a communication breakdown. Using the communication model, can you analyze what went wrong, why, and how you might have fixed the problem?

9. We've all done *content analysis* (e.g., a book or film review), and when we do, what we're really looking at are the *messages* in the media. And when you shop for Christmas presents you're really doing *audience analysis* (what gift is appropriate for Aunt Jenny or your best friend?). It's the same process that the media use to study their intended *audience.*

   Each part of the communication process, in fact, has a parallel type of analysis to go with it. Can you identify which types of analysis occur with the *sender, channel,* and *feedback* elements? Give examples.

Chapter 1: True/False Test

The Nature and Function of Mass Communication Systems

1. How receivers respond to messages may depend on several things, such as their surroundings, emotions, educational level, and cultural background.

2. Feedback *guarantees* that your audience understood your message exactly as you meant it.

3. Not communicating with someone, giving him/her the "silent treatment," *is* a message in itself.

4. Raising your hand in class is a message in itself.

5. Test grades are examples of feedback.

6. Television and Hollywood often enjoy symbiotic relationships.

7. Sending a birthday card is a machine-assisted form of interpersonal communication.

8. Only mass media sources, not audiences, can be gatekeepers.

9. Deciding what kind of clothes to wear (for a date, class, or job interview) is a communication encoding decision in itself.

10. Semantic noise starts when a receiver decodes the meaning of a message differently than the source intended it to be decoded.

11. Two people who view the same message in different ways create a symbiotic relationship.

12. Cable television has yet to fractionalize its content offerings.

13. Communication is to *channel* as process is to *tool*.

14. Because of the size and complexity of the mass media, individual feedback is impossible.

15. You plead with your instructor for more time to do your term paper. He/she understands your request, but still says "No." By definition, you've thereby failed to communicate.

Chapter 1: Multiple Choice Test

The Nature and Function of Mass Communication Systems

1. Spelling errors, radio static, and fuzzy pictures are examples of:

   a. semantic noise
   b. a facsimile

   c. mechanical noise
   d. symbiosis

2. When two people or groups argue over different versions of "the truth" (as each sees it), this is really a problem in:

   a. environmental noise
   b. semantic noise

   c. gatekeeping
   d. feedback response

3. The process by which media workers decide what will and won't get into the media is called:

   a. decoding
   b. feedback looping

   c. fractionalization
   d. gatekeeping

4. Which one of these items *doesn't* fit the profile of a mass media audience?

   a. audience members generally select themselves
   b. they are demographically "alike"
   c. members are usually geographically scattered
   d. audiences are large in number

5. Which one of these items *doesn't* fit the profile of a mass media source?

   a. most exist primarily to make a profit
   b. usually part of a larger, formal organization
   c. generally operate with multiple gatekeepers
   d. rarely risk competition with similar organizations

6. Trying to talk to a friend at a music concert would likely require overcoming _____ noise.

   a. mechanical
   b. environmental

   c. semantic
   d. all the above

7. An interpersonal message could be encoded to be decoded in _____ physical senses.

   a. two
   b. three
   c. four
   d. five

8. Most of us "experience" television through how many physical senses?

   a. one
   b. two
   c. three
   d. five

9. Mass media *fragmentation* breaks content into smaller, more precisely defined pieces; *convergence* brings the distribution, content, and hardware formats of mass media closer together.

   a. true
   b. false

10. Talking with someone on a cellular phone illustrates:

    a. intrapersonal communication
    b. interpersonal communication
    c. interpersonal communication, machine-assisted
    d. mass communication

11. That you can understand this question means that you're able to _____ this message.

    a. encode
    b. decode
    c. receive
    d. feedback

12. Communication models (or any theoretical model) help us do all the following *except:*

    a. organize, order, and relate various concepts to one another
    b. explain things by illustrating them in simplified form
    c. guarantee successful results by following model processes
    d. predict outcomes

13. What force(s) are driving the process of media fragmentation?

    a. individual special interests
    b. changing audience demographics
    c. increasing demands on personal time
    d. all the above

14. Mass media communication is becoming increasingly:

    a. complex   c. fragmented
    b. fragile   d. all the above

15. When deciding what facts to report and which not to, journalists exercise the _____ element of communications.

    a. noise reduction   c. gatekeeping
    b. symbiosis   d. feedback

16. A mass communications audience begins with how many people?

    a. 25   c. 1,000
    b. 100   d. no set number above two

17. Which of these industries pairs has the *least* symbiotic relationship?

    a. radio and music   c. newspaper and advertising
    b. film and television   d. book and music

18. Reading the latest issue of *Sports Illustrated* via Prodigy (an on-line computer database) is an example of media:

    a. segmentation   c. convergence
    b. fragmentation   d. none of the above

19. Individual feedback in mass communications is likely to be:

    a. delayed   c. indirect
    b. inconvenient   d. all the above

20. Mass media organizations tend to be:

    a. highly organized   c. bureaucratic
    b. predictable   d. all the above

CHAPTER 1:   TEST ANSWER KEYS

True/False Test

01. True	05. True	09. True	13. True
02. False	06. True	10. True	14. False
03. True	07. True	11. False	15. False
04. True	08. False	12. False	

Multiple-Choice Test

01. C	06. B	11. B	16. D
02. B	07. D	12. C	17. D
03. D	08. B	13. D	18. C
04. B	09. A	14. D	19. D
05. D	10. C	15. C	20. D

-------------- N O T E S --------------

Chapter 2

Uses and Functions of Mass Communications

With this chapter we discover the various perspectives from which we can analyze mass communications, selecting the functional approach as perhaps the most useful. This approach states simply that something is best understood by examining how it's used. As such, we'll take a wide-scope look at the five major functions that mass communications provides to our society; conversely, we'll then focus on the four functions the media provides individuals--each of the functions having its own distinct strengths and weaknesses.

CHAPTER OBJECTIVES

.   understand how the mass media functions by analyzing the various ways society and individuals need and use the media

.   analyze the inherent benefits and risks of using mass media

KEY TERMS AND CONCEPTS

[ ] functional approach to studying mass communications (definition); [ ] dysfunctions
[ ] **how society uses the mass media (macroanalytic view)**
   [ ] surveillance (informative role)
     [ ] warning (beware-of-threats) surveillance
     [ ] instrumental surveillance (useful information)
     [ ] media credibility
     [ ] status conferral
   [ ] interpretation (viewpoint role)
   [ ] linkage (connective role)
   [ ] transmission of values (socialization role)
   [ ] entertainment (diversionary role)
   [ ] uses-and-gratifications model
[ ] **how individuals use the mass media (microanalytic view)**
   [ ] cognition (to understand both topical *and* general knowledge)
   [ ] diversion: [ ] stimulation; [ ] relaxation; [ ] emotional release (catharsis)
   [ ] social utility, types of: [ ] conversational currency; [ ] parasocial relationships
   [ ] withdrawal

TOPICS FOR DISCUSSION

1. What types of movies do you generally watch? Have your tastes changed over the last four years? If so, how? Why?

2. Do you know anyone who often "escapes" into the media (including on-line computer services)?

3. Have you ever averted a dangerous situation, either directly or indirectly, due to what you heard, saw, or read in the media?

4. What social and personal values currently portrayed in the media do you agree or disagree with?

5. Have you ever tried to contact any medium because of the values or lifestyles it presented which you wanted to encourage, modify, or stop?

6. Do you believe that there were any dysfunctional consequences of media coverage of the O.J. Simpson trial? Can you support your position with more than just opinion?

7. Have you ever gained useful or significant knowledge (instrumental surveillance) from a Hollywood film? Are newer movies more valuable in that regard than pre-1980 films?

8. Which mass medium do you feel delivers the best overall perspective on current events? Why? Do you have a favorite media personality with whom you usually agree? Do you ever seek out different points of view? If not, why not?

9. Relate an event in which the linkage function did or didn't benefit you. Have you ever sought out (or been sought by) a particular group? Is junk mail linkage? Telemarketing?

10. Andy Warhol once said that everyone will become famous for at least fifteen minutes once in his or her lifetime. Has the media ever confirmed "status" on you--by accident or design?

11. Most people find TV news more credible than newspapers. Do you agree? Why or why not?

12. Do you think films routinely cater to the least common denominator of public taste? Whatever you answer, do you see that as an increasing or a decreasing trend?

Chapter 2: True/False Test

Uses and Functions of Mass Communications

1. A wide-angle investigation is to a narrow one what macroanalysis is to microanalysis.

2. The "functional" approach to exploring mass communications holds that something is best understood by examining how it is used.

3. Since mass communication is a passive activity it can never cause harm to individuals.

4. A movie can entertain us or warn us (warning surveillance) of impending threats (e.g. deadly viruses, danger from terrorists, and so on), but it can't do both at the same time.

5. Status conferral is a one-way process; you can get it, but you can't get it simply by asking for it.

6. Political cartoons generally serve the *interpretative function* of the mass media.

7. A long-time "soap" fan has proabably formed parasocial relationships with the show's characters.

8. When seller meets buyer through a classified ad, they've both experienced mass communication's "linkage" function.

9. To make mass media entertainment that offers both widespread appeal and high profits, critics contend that producers must usually appeal to the lower common denominators of public taste.

10. Our understanding of how and why people use the media (and what they get from it) comes mostly from scientific laboratory experiments.

11. The word *cognition* means "coming to know something."

12. Hallucination seems to be the by-product of sensory deprivation; put another way, if there's nothing else going on in your environment, you'll eventually create your own private world.

13. Any medium is capable of producing "sensory overload."

14. Advertisements often help set (or at least transmit) our collective cultural values.

15. *Conversational currency* is a term used to describe the costs involved in those 1-900 sex/ romance/party phone services.

Chapter 2: Multiple-Choice Test

Uses and Functions of Mass Communications

1. Studying mass communications by understanding how they're used is called the _____ approach.

    a. persuasive
    b. effectual
    c. functional
    d. pervasive

2. Undesirable consequences of mass media usage are called:

    a. dysfunctions
    b. mishaps
    c. cataclysms
    d. adversities

3. When the media warn you of an impending danger, you benefit from the _____ function of mass communications.

    a. linkage
    b. surveillance
    c. socialization
    d. interpretation

4. As mass media took over the roles of tribal sentry, troubadour, and historian, some significant changes began occurring. Which of these wasn't one of those changes?

    a. the range of events that concerned or interested us increased
    b. our ability to directly verify news reports increased
    c. news and information now travels faster and further
    d. multiple news sources erased the likelihood of misinformation

5. Generally conceded to be the most important asset a newspaper has is its:

    a. format
    b. credibility
    c. postal privileges
    d. size

6. About the only thing status conferral *guarantees* is:

    a. expertise
    b. popularity
    c. short-lived prominence
    d. a leadership role

7. If you consistently rely on only one source of news information or interpretation, which of the below effects is probably the *most* likely consequence?

    a. your perspective sharpens
    b. your ability to make balanced judgments increases
    c. the likelihood of making mistakes decreases
    d. none of the above

8. The interpretative function of mass media provides all but:

    a. opinions
    b. analysis

    c. perspectives
    d. catharsis

9. If you rely too much on one newspaper's editorials, one TV news program's analysis, or one "expert" commentator, you might risk:

    a. getting an unbalanced viewpoint
    b. losing the ability to think for yourself

    c. a loss of perspective
    d. all the above

10. Of the five societal functions provided by mass media, the most pervasive is the _____ function.

    a. surveillance
    b. interpretive

    c. entertainment
    d. transmission of values

11. Late-night TV talk shows best illustrate the _____ role of the mass media.

    a. surveillance
    b. linkage

    c. transmission of values
    d. all the above

12. Not smoking, saying no to drugs, or practicing safe sex exemplify how the mass media can help reinforce new social values. This illustrates the _____ role of mass meida on a societal level.

    a. withdrawal
    b. socialization

    c. parasocial
    d. all the above

13. "Escaping" in a book (on a habitual basis) illustrates the _____ function of the uses-and-gratification theory.

    a. conversational currency
    b. linkage

    c. withdrawal
    d. parasocial

16

14. Apparently the one condition that few human beings can tolerate very well is:

    a. extensive boredom
    b. media withdrawal
    c. stimulation
    d. prominence

15. In terms of total hours broadcast, TV primarily serves the _____ function on both the social and individual levels.

    a. persuasive
    b. entertainment
    c. surveillance
    d. linkage

16. Strangers can usually strike up a conversation about Jay Leno, the Chicago Bulls, or *Apollo 13*. This phenomenon is made possible by using the media as:

    a. conversational currency
    b. a withdrawal device
    c. a parasocial relationship
    d. none of the above

17. Parasocial media relationships are usually:

    a. one-sided
    b. loneliness diversions
    c. audience-created
    d. all the above

18. Crying, laughing, screaming: these can all be the by-product of emotional release. Aristotle called this phenomenon:

    a. catharsis
    b. cosmos
    c. utilitarianism
    d. chaos

19. The uses-and-gratification approach to the analysis of mass media usage is:

    a. a verifiable fact
    b. a hypothesis

20. What distinguishes the motives of a person using the media for diversion versus withdrawal?

    a. diversion is a way to "get away from it all" on a temporary basis; withdrawal tends to be more antisocial and long term
    b. diversion is a sure sign of immaturity; withdrawal isn't
    c. diversion is unhealthy escapism; withdrawal is simply a temporary mental vacation
    d. nothing; the underlying motives are identical

CHAPTER 2: TEST ANSWER KEYS

True/False Test

01. True	05. True	09. True	13. False
02. True	06. True	10. False	14. True
03. False	07. True	11. True	15. False
04. False	08. True	12. True	

Multiple-Choice Test

01. C	06. C	11. C	16. A
02. A	07. D	12. B	17. D
03. B	08. D	13. C	18. A
04. B	09. D	14. A	19. B
05. B	10. D	15. B	20. A

-------------- N O T E S --------------

Chapter 3

The Global Village:
International and Comparative Mass Media Systems

In order to appreciate how mass media function in a particular society or country, we must first understand how the government views its role relative to its people (and the press). At one extreme, authoritarian governments attempt to put limits on the mass media by controlling what information does and does not reach the public; in a very real sense, the government becomes the ultimate gatekeeper. On the other end of the spectrum, democratic governments may pay relatively little regulatory attention to media content; in this sense, the government pays homage to the idea that intelligent people are quite capable of making up their own minds about controversial issues.

This chapter explores the diverse ways these opposing philosophies (and hybrid mixtures) shape the role and function of mass media throughout the globe. In a world of industrialized versus developing nations, the values embodied by one country's film and TV media may be just as effective--and just as unwelcome--as an invading army.

CHAPTER OBJECTIVES

.   recognize how a quickly emerging mass media system is effectively "melting" national borders on a global basis, allowing entertainment, news, and information to flow between once-diverse cultures at both an escalating rate and depth.

.   observe the variety of ways mass media are controlled, financed, and operated in other countries, largely paralleling the philosophical relationship between the government and the governed

KEY TERMS AND CONCEPTS

[ ] global village; [ ] trends in global print and broadcast media
[ ] the mass media's impact on the changing world political scene
[ ] cultural domination (cf. "spillover programming")
[ ] theories of the press
    [ ] authoritarianism; [ ] communist; [ ] libertarianism;
    [ ] social responsibility; [ ] developmental
[ ] media operations as distinguished by:
    [ ] *control* (centralized versus decentralized)
    [ ] *ownership* (public vs. private)
[ ] New World Order; [ ] UNESCO and the "free press" debate

TOPICS FOR DISCUSSION

1. In the world of *Star Trek*, its most important governing principle, the "Prime Directive" forbids twenty-third-century explorers from interfering in the development of a foreign culture (even if done with good intentions). Should we adopt a similar policy toward other nations in regard to infusing our values into their cultures via our mass media? Do they have a right to develop the way they want, even if their development goes counter to our deepest held values?

2. Forty years ago the term *Ugly American* symbolized us as a people unconcerned with any other culture but our own. But have we changed? Do you ever seek out foreign television programs, films, books, or music that reflect a different political, religious, or entertainment viewpoint?

3. In many countries a shortwave radio is as common as VCRs are in the U.S. Why do you suppose shortwave radio sets are so uncommon here?

4. What are the pros and cons--as far as you're concerned--of living in a "global village?"

5. The ideals of libertarianism gave birth to our First Amendment; government, it decrees, has no business regulating free speech or the press. Do you agree? Are there some subjects or ideas that we shouldn't tolerate? What about people who promote racism, sexism, antisemitism, drugs, communism, pornography, or war? Should the First Amendment be absolute and untouchable?

6. If you wanted to buy a foreign newspaper or magazine, rent a foreign film, or listen to an international broadcast, how far would you have to go from home to do it? Conclusions?

7. What's wrong, if anything, with the idea that mass media should mandatorily serve the government's goal of improving the education, health, and material well-being of its citizens?

8. If you've visited other countries, describe the differences you observed between their media (and cultural values) and ours.

9. What can we do to increase our understanding of other cultures? Or do we even need to?

10. Since the U.S. is the only superpower left, some people suggest that it's up to other cultures to learn more about us, not vice versa. Do you agree?

11. Should we have a government-sponsored national newspaper or magazine? What about a radio and television network? What about on a global level? Why or why not?

Chapter 3: True/False Test
International and Comparative Mass Media Systems

1. The term *global village* suggests a world in which the economies, cultures and well being of all nations are becoming inextricably interrelated and interdependent because of communication ties.

2. Most governments still prohibit foreign media to be distributed within their borders.

3. Geopolitical borders continue to be an impenetrable barrier to mass communications.

4. Of the various mass media operating philosophies, libertarianism is the least restrictive.

5. There are no newspapers or television programs distributed on a world-wide basis.

6. The biggest change in international broadcasting during the last fifteen years has been the increased use of communication satellites to carry TV signals acrosss national borders.

7. Even though the U.S. is a major entertainment media exporter, our profits from international film and TV program sales continue to be rather slim.

8. The trend in global media ownership is toward smaller, regionally isolated corporations.

9. A major concern of countries that import U.S. media is that they'll become "Americanized" with our own particular brand of cultural, political and moral values.

10. Though U.S. TV is very popular oversees, the highest-rated shows are still produced locally.

11. It's been suggested that the global democratic movement triumphed over authoritarian nations by, in part, transmitting its cultural values via entertainment such as movies and TV, and thereby undermining the existing political and cultural values of the importing nations.

12. Nations whose people speak different languages don't have to worry about potentially adverse effects from "spillover programming."

13. In the eyes of developing nations, traditional Western media entertainment and news coverage is like a form of media colonialism.

13. In the eyes of developing nations, the "New World Order" is like a form of media colonialism.

14. Reporters in the West agree that their news reports about developing nations tend to be biased and unbalanced, and therefore concur that journalists reporting there should be "licensed."

15. Some developing nations believe the press has a philosophical obligation to support government policies, help supress dissent, and assist in achieving national goals.

Chapter 3:   Multiple-Choice Test

The Global Village:

International and Comparative Mass Media Systems

1. What concerns countries who rely heavily on U.S. media for entertainment is their fear of:

    a. too much U.S. advertising
    b. U.S. cultural domination
    c. political revolution
    d. all the above

2. Who popularized the concept of the "global village?"

    a. George Bush
    b. Marshall McLuhan
    c. UNESCO
    d. *World* magazine

3. An expansion in worldwide communications suggests that there should also be a parallel trend and increase in worldwide _____ .

    a. conversational currency
    b. common values
    c. international deregulation
    d. none of the above

4. Almost all U.S. mass media is popular, but which of the following pairs dominates world sales?

    a. books and magazines
    b. radio and television
    c. films and records
    d. advertising and newspapers

5. _____ dominate the international flow of news.

    a. American newspapers
    b. authoritarian governments
    c. global news agencies
    d. East Asian multinational corporations

6. Most large-scale, shortwave radio programs are:

    a. state supported
    b. interlaced with propaganda
    c. used for political purposes
    d. all the above

7. In which of these countries has the government succeeded (for now, at least) in continuing to suppress large-scale access to foreign mass media?

   a. China
   b. Egypt

   c. Germany
   d. Bosnia

8. The term *global village* refers to the:

   a. concept of a one-government world
   b. elimination of international trade barriers
   c. concept that everyone on the planet, thanks to mass media, is becoming interconnected with, and dependent upon, one another
   d. the "brave new-world" concept made popular by UNESCO

9. Most foreign newspapers imported into a country are:

   a. profit losers
   b. printed in Spanish

   c. targeted to a traveler's home country
   d. owned by Time-Warner, Inc.

10. Typical methods used by authoritarian nations to force their will on their press have included all but which of the below:

    a. licensing
    b. journalism school closures

    c. censorship
    d. harsh, physical punishments

MATCH THE NEXT FOUR QUESTIONS WITH THE BELOW ANSWERS

   a. authoritarian
   b. developmental

   c. libertarian
   d. social responsibility

11. This theory holds that citizens are rational people capable of making intelligent decisions when informed of both sides of an issue; citizens therefore insist on freedom of speech. Government, they believe, serves best when it interferes least.

12. Government leaders know what's best for its citizens; the media, therefore, exist to serve the interests of the government. In this elitist society, government serves best when it guides most.

13. In this society, the press exists primarily to serve national economic and social goals.

14. This press system maintains that while the press must be free of most governmental controls, it has an obligation to respond to the interests and needs of its parent society.

15. The growth of democracy and the growing popularity of free marketplace economics have resulted in more countries endorsing the _____ approach to press regulation.

   a. authoritarian
   b. developmental

   c. social responsibility
   d. libertarian

16. Which country below still operates under the communist theory?

   a. Costa Rica
   b. Iraq

   c. Iran
   d. Peoples Republic of China

17. The press system of any nation reflects:

   a. the developmental theory of mass media systems
   b. libertarian ideals
   c. a society that demands a socially responsible structure
   d. the social and political system of that nation

18. The document that inhibits our government from infringing upon freedom of the press is the:

   a. Magna Carta
   b. First Amendment

   c. Declaration of Independence
   d. Articles of Confederation

19. Developmental journalism is closest in philosophy to which of these press theories?

   a. libertarianism
   b. social responsibility

   c. authoritarianism
   d. communist

20. Which of the below countries does not fit the "public-centralized" typology of media ownership and control?

   a. France
   b. Peoples Republic of China

   c. North Korea
   d. Cuba

CHAPTER 3: TEST ANSWER KEYS

True/False Test

01. True	05. False	09. True	13. True
02. False	06. True	10. True	14. False
03. False	07. False	11. False	15. True
04. True	08. True	12. True	

Multiple-Choice Test

01. B	06. D	11. C	16. D
02. B	07. A	12. A	17. D
03. A	08. C	13. B	18. B
04. B	09. B	14. D	19. C
05. C	10. B	15. A	20. A

-------------- N O T E S --------------

Chapter 4

History of the Print Media

This chapter reviews the history of Western printing, centering our attention on the evolution of American newspapers, magazines, and books. We'll also examine the personalities, motives, and technological breakthroughs that led to the sophisticated level of print media we enjoy today.

CHAPTER OBJECTIVES

- trace the emergence of press styles, audiences, and press functions in the United States

- understand the technological, social, and economic forces that led to the development of mass audiences for the print media; learn how and why those same factors have continued to encourage an evolution in the content and operations in today's publishing industries

KEY TERMS AND CONCEPTS

[ ] Johann Gutenberg and his moveable-type printing press; [ ] publishing "under authority"
[ ] Benjamin and James Franklin (their contributions to the colonial press)
[ ] John Peter Zenger trial, 1733; [ ] Stamp Act of 1765, issues behind
[ ] political (partisan) press, characteristics of
[ ] *magazine*, early content characteristics
[ ] First Amendment (the various freedoms guaranteed)
[ ] Sedition Act, connection to press freedom (cf. Federalist vs. anti-Federalist movements)
[ ] mass produced newspapers, developments necessary for
[ ] the penny press, characteristics and significance of
[ ] the role of schools and libraries in promoting literacy (thereby promoting publishing)
[ ] the "lead" and the "inverted pyramid," significance of these news writing techniques
[ ] journalistic innovations of: [ ] Joseph Pulitzer; [ ] E. W. Scripps; [ ] Wm. Randolph Hearst
[ ] yellow journalism (sensationalism); [ ] muckrakers
[ ] reasons for newspaper consolidation in the early 20th century
[ ] jazz journalism, characteristics of; [ ] tabloid newspaper
[ ] reasons for the rise in popularity of magazines and paperback books between 1860 - 1900
[ ] impact of the Great Depression on newspapers and reporting; [ ] interpretive reporting
[ ] major developments in the post-World War I magazine industry
[ ] major economic influences and effects on newspapers, magazines, and books, 1945-1969
[ ] underground press; [ ] investigative reporting; [ ] precision journalism
[ ] innovations of *USA Today* on modern newspapers

TOPICS FOR DISCUSSION

1. Having seen the various approaches to reporting that American journalism has undergone, do you see any ways for improvement?

2. Should American newspapers advocate or avoid partisan positions?

3. Is there any muckraking in today's media--print or broadcast?

4. Why is the concept of "big is better" perhaps okay for newspaper readership, but not necessarily for magazines?

5. Most other countries have always had a "national" newspaper; why do you think we took so long to develop a non-financial one?

6. The original reason we created the newspaper "lead" and "inverted pyramid" writing style during the Civil War has obviously disappeared; but has the *utility* of that style become obsolete?

7. Do you see modern-day descendants of sensationalism or yellow journalism in any of today's print media?

8. What's wrong, if anything, with a bit of sensationalism as long as the information given is factual?

9. Describe (using examples) the difference between interpretive and investigative journalism. Is either inherently better? Should the techniques of precision journalism be encouraged?

10. Critics once called *USA Today* a "McPaper;" some even suggest we needed a new Pulitzer prize category for the "Best Written Paragraph of the Year." What advantages or disadvantages do you see in *USA Today's* super concise style--or their use of factoids?

11. Book industry critics scorn today's publishers for encouraging mass-appeal books over higher-quality works with limited appeal. Do you see any support for those views?

12. Explain the difference between mass paperbacks and quality paperbacks. Which type dominates your home library?

13. Over 98 percent of American cities have no competing daily newspapers. Is that dangerous? Are other media taking up the slack by offering differing viewpoints in the same market area?

14. Do you see any need for an underground press in our society?

15. Since newspapers are big business, why shouldn't the government tax them just as the British tried in the Stamp Act of 1765?

Chapter 4: True/False Test

History of the Print Media

1. Johann Gutenberg introduced books and the printing press around 1750.

2. Publishing "under authority" meant that an author was a certified expert in a given subject area.

3. Press censorship essentially began with the introduction of the moveable-type printing press.

4. The only "news" the penny press and the era's magazines avoided were social "crusade" issues.

5. Colonial papers were widely recognized for objective reporting and balanced political views.

6. Colonial publishers targeted their newspapers, books, and magazines at an affluent and well-educated audience.

7. Jazz journalism papers, noted for their tabloid size, stressed photographic news coverage.

8. The penny press changed the primary method of newspaper distribution from mail delivery to street sales.

9. Woodcut engravings were forerunners to photographs.

10. Most newspapers are regional in focus, while most magazines aim at national audiences.

11. *Precision journalism* is a relatively new reporting technique that uses social science research methods, such as polling, in order to provide unique insights and greater depth to news stories.

12. Yellow journalism appeals to reader emotion rather than reader intellect.

13. Theodore Roosevelt attached the term *muckrakers* to writers who crusaded against the social abuses of big business.

14. The United States still does not have a "national" newspaper.

15. Although immensely popular, *USA Today* has failed to have much of an innovative impact on other American newspapers.

Chapter 4:   Multiple-Choice Test

History of the Print Media

1. Which of the subjects below wasn't of particular interest to people when mass-produced books and newspapers first began?

    a. commercial news
    b. religious issues
    c. foreign, political, and war news
    d. adventure-based fiction

2. *USA Today* started several major developments in publishing. Which of these doesn't belong?

    a. short, easily digested stories
    b. extensive use of graphs, charts, tables, and statistics
    c. a heavy use of in-depth investigative stories
    d. the use of factoids

3. The introduction of mass-produced print media in the fifteenth and sixteenth centuries produced all but which of these effects:

    a. people wanted to be more educated; universities expanded
    b. freedom of speech and press flourished
    c. curiosity fueled demand for news and information
    d. printing became a widespread and profitable industry

4. The term *underground press*, coined in the 1960s, refers to a type of reporting best described as:

    a. anti-establishment
    b. apartheid
    c. abolitionist
    d. none of the above

5. Three distinct magazine types emerged between WW I and WW II; which doesn't belong?

    a. the digest
    b. sex-oriented magazines
    c. the news weekly
    d. the pictorial magazine

6. Which of these would you *least* likely see in the penny press?

    a. crime stories
    b. human interest features
    c. political speeches
    d. sports and business news

7. The _____ hastened the drive toward American independence.

   a. John Peter Zenger trial   c. Bill of Rights
   b. the Stamp Act of 1765   d. *Boston News Letter*

8. Identify the false statement. The penny press introduced the idea that news:

   a. was a commodity--the fresher, the better
   b. should be gathered in the fastest possible way
   c. was an activity that demanded professional news gatherers (reporters)
   d. should be aimed at the affluent, well-educated, and politically savvy upper class

9. Modern magazines might *best* be described as:

   a. favoring specialized content   c. pioneering multimedia effects
   b. preferring less graphics and more print   d. becoming more regionalized

10. The First Amendment does *not* address this freedom:

    a. press   c. speech
    b. right to bear arms   d. religion

11. He began the *North Star* newspaper, became an elegant speaker for the repeal of slavery, and helped raise an all-black Civil War regiment (the film *Glory* recounts the story).

    a. Joseph Pulitzer   c. Frederick Douglass
    b. Horatio Alger   d. Mark Twain

12. Which of these was *not* a prevailing practice during the Pulitzer-Scripps-Hearst era?

    a. sold newspaper space according to circulation figures
    b. emphasized clean page makeup and a simple-to-read writing style
    c. used attention-getting stunts to promote readership
    d. kept newspaper reporting objective by avoiding sensationalism

13. Which answer below was *not* one of the elements necessary for the success of mass-produced newspapers in the 1830s?

    a. quick, cost-effective printing presses   c. widespread literacy
    b. the advent of copyright laws   d. a rising middle class, or mass audience

30

14. Which of these was *not* an innovation made during the Pulitzer-Scripps-Hearst era?

    a. newspaper chains introduced
    b. *precision journalism* introduced
    c. frequent crusades for the working class begun
    d. sensationalized news introduced to up readership

15. Reasons for the decline in the number of newspapers during the early part of the 20th century include all but which of the following:

    a. increased production costs
    b. marked advertiser preference for larger circulation newspapers
    c. a trend toward standardized content (made possible by syndication)
    d. tighter enforcement of federal anti-trust laws against chain newspapers

16. Which of these did *not* account for the big increase in magazine popularity between 1860-1900.

    a. passage of the Ninth Amendment
    b. more efficient printing techniques
    c. a national audience
    d. Postal Act of 1879 (introduces 2nd class rates)

17. All these statements about early paperback books are true *except:*

    a. popularity began during Civil War
    b. popular for their heavy use of pictures
    c. stressed ideals of virtue, hard work, and courage
    d. content often pirated from European best sellers

18. The trend toward newspaper consolidation in the early twentieth century was furthered along by:

    a. federal antitrust legislation
    b. new technologies which made publishing an expensive business
    c. advertisers who preferred big circulation newspapers
    d. standardized content that made multiple newspapers redundant

19. Idenitfy the false statement. The penny press changed how:

    a. newspapers were licensed
    b. news was defined
    c. newspapers were distributed and financed
    d. news was collected and reported

20. Johann Gutenberg invented:

    a. the book
    b. the newspaper
    c. moveable type
    d. woodcut engravings

31

CHAPTER 4: TEST ANSWER KEYS

True/False Test

01. False	05. False	09. True	13. True
02. False	06. True	10. True	14. False
03. True	07. True	11. True	15. False
04. False	08. True	12. True	

Multiple-Choice Test

01. D	06. C	11. C	16. A
02. C	07. B	12. D	17. B
03. B	08. D	13. B	18. A
04. A	09. A	14. B	19. A
05. B	10. B	15. D	20. C

-------------- **N O T E S** --------------

Chapter 5

Structure of the Newspaper Industry

This chapter surveys the emergence of the "new" newspaper, designed to attract new readers by tailoring content and format to the wants and needs of a visually oriented and time-starved society. We'll examine how a typical newspaper is put together and the roles of key players in a newspaper office. At the end we'll consider the emerging solutions--and problems--in ownership patterns, production technology, and the potential conflict between editorial and business interests.

CHAPTER OBJECTIVES

. recognize the variety of newspaper types by their publishing frequency and market audience

. examine current trends in newspaper ownership, technology, and production techniques

. consider the philosophical and economic issues raised by advances in digital technology, in business operations, and in the pursuit of giving readers and advertisers what they want

KEY TERMS AND CONCEPTS

[ ] print newspaper categories: publication frequency: [ ] market size; [ ] special interest appeal
[ ] circulation = [ ] subscription + [ ] newsstand sales
[ ] national newspapers (characteristics and distribution methods)
[ ] large metropolitan dailies (general status and trends); [ ] zoned editions
[ ] suburban and small-town dailies (general status and trends)
[ ] weeklies (characteristics of; advantages over dailies)
[ ] newspaper strategies to recapture readers: color, writing, content, and audience feedback
[ ] special-service and minority papers, profiles: [ ] ethnic; [ ] college; [ ] shoppers
[ ] online newspapers, characteristics of (advantages and disadvantages over print media)
[ ] newspaper ownership trends: [ ] consolidation and [ ] single-market declining competition
    [ ] chains; [ ] joint-operating agreement (JOA)
[ ] group ownership, pros and cons
[ ] roles of publisher and editors (managing, wire, city, and copy); [ ] beat reporters
[ ] newspaper departments: business, production, news-editorial
[ ] newspaper revenue sources: [ ] advertising, four types; [ ] circulation, two types
[ ] newshole, advertising-to-editorial typical space ratio

TOPICS FOR DISCUSSION

1. What implications do you draw from the fact that proportionately fewer Americans are reading newspapers today?

2. Why don't newspapers seem to appeal to the under-30 crowd? Do they interest you?

3. Examine your own newspaper reading habits. Which types do you read, how often, and why? What could newspapers do to improve their appeal to you?

4. What are the strengths and weaknesses of your college newspaper? Does it serve the entire student body or only a targeted elite group?

5. The so-called "reader-driven" newspaper attempts to give readers the types of stories they want; what inherent dangers, if any, do you see in this philosophy?

6. Have you ever seen an online newspaper? What were your impressions? What advantages and disadvantages did you note?

7. Why do more affluent neighborhoods generally have more newspapers from which to choose? Is it simply a matter of affordability?

8. Are newspapers, as we know them, obsolete? If we can get news, features, and advertisements from computer databases (such as CompuServe or Prodigy), why bother with paper?

9. From an environmental standpoint, can we continue to afford newspapers (consider the trees used for pulp and all the paper that *isn't* recycled)?

10. Is your paper fragmented into separate sections for specific purposes? Which of those sections do you find most useful?

11. If you could do without specific sections (and other readers likewise), why can't newspapers save you time (and themselves money) by giving you only the sections you want?

12. Are newspapers in your area independently or chain operated? How many of each are there?

13. If sensationalism worked so well in the 1800s, should today's publishers give it another try?

14. Have you ever seen a religious newspaper? A prison paper? An underground newspaper? What other special-interest groups can you think of that have their own paper?

15. What's wrong, if anything, with having an "official" government newspaper? Or one operated by your state, town, or college?

Chapter 5: True/False Test

Structure of the Newspaper Industry

1. Fewer people read newspapers today (relative to growing population figures) than ever before.

2. One reason for declining newspaper ad revenue is that advertisers now have a wider choice of media outlets from which to choose.

3. Subscription = circulation + newsstand sales

4. National newspapers are printed in a central plant, then flown overnight throughout the nation.

5. A "zoned edition" is one technique big city newspapers use to compete in the suburban market.

6. There are twice as many daily newspapers in the U.S. as weeklies.

7. Weekly newspapers have two major advantages over their big city cousins: the ability to report more closely on their readership, and the ability to offer advertisers more precise local exposure at cheaper prices than big city papers.

8. Growth in Sunday newspaper sales suggests that people will read more if they have the time.

9. "Shoppers," or "pennysavers" are not considered newspapers since they don't carry news.

10. Online, newspapers give you more advertising but less news than their regular print editions.

11. Fewer and fewer U.S. cities have competing daily newspapers.

12. The person who determines overall policy of a newspaper is the managing editor.

13. A paper that's one of several owned by the same parent company is called a "chain" newspaper.

14. Advertisements typically account for about 40 percent of newspaper space.

15. Typically, more and more newspapers are offering what they call "reader-driven" content, i.e., stories on issues or subjects about which readers say they want or need to know.

Chapter 5:   Multiple Choice Test

Structure of the Newspaper Industry

1. Newspapers have fallen on lean times recently; which of these *isn't* one of the reasons?

   a. falling ad revenues due to competition with other media
   b. increasing competition for their readers' time
   c. decreasing reader interest in self-help and feature stories
   d. continuing trouble in attracting the under-30 reader

2. Which of the below is not a type of newspaper advertising?

   a. infomercial   c. preprints
   b. national   d. classified

3. Which newspaper group has been hardest hit by circulation slides?

   a. national   c. large metro dailies
   b. suburban weeklies   d. small-town dailies

4. Which of these is *not* a national newspaper?

   a. Prodigy   c. *USA Today*
   b. *Christian Science Monitor*   d. *Wall Street Journal*

5. Newspapers are trying to recapture readers with several strategies; which doesn't belong?

   a. using more color and graphics   c. writing shorter, punchier stories
   b. offering more "lifestyle" features   d. featuring more in-depth and complex stories

6. Which of these is *not* a criticism of group newspapers?

   a. publishers are "absentee owners" with little knowledge about the communities they serve
   b. group newspapers' larger profits can provide better services that independents can't
   c. owners may avoid controversy to preclude irritating advertisers
   d. fewer competing papers means a loss in the diversity of available opinions

7. Newspapers are especially trying to get more readers from which of these groups?

   a. ethnic minorities   c. suburban empty nesters
   b. people under 30   d. upper-income families

8. Who would typically write police, fire, education, or local political stories?

   a. copy editor   c. beat reporter
   b. city desk   d. wire editor

9. Which of the below is *not* typically an advantage of an online newspaper?

   a. portability   c. more available information
   b. quick information search capabilities   d. easier, greater reader interactivity

10. The person in charge of a paper's day-to-day operations is the:

   a. managing editor   c. city editor
   b. wire editor   d. publisher

11. How many pages a newspaper publishes normally depends on the:

   a. circulation size   c. advertising volume
   b. amount of available news   d. consumer demand

12. Advertising revenue accounts for about _____ percent of a newspaper's total profits.

   a. 20   c. 60
   b. 40   d. 80

13. How much a paper charges for advertising space is determined by:

   a. total circulation   c. the day of the week
   b. number of subscribers   d. fixed rates set by National Ad Council

14. Which type of newspaper advertising typically brings in the greatest volume of money?

   a. national   c. preprint
   b. local   d. classified

15. Which of these is *not* true about joint-operating agreements?

    a. JOAs must be approved by the U.S. Department of Justice
    b. only the advertising staffs remain separate and competitive
    c. purpose: help retain two newspaper voices in the same city
    d. saves money by legally combining operational costs

16. A *newshole* is:

    a. a beat reporter's informant
    b. slang term for online news space
    c. space available for news depending on ad volume
    d. space reserved for late-breaking stories

17. Which medium leads in total advertising revenues?

    a. newspapers
    b. radio
    c. television
    d. magazines

18. Which of these newspaper groups has suffered the biggest circulation declines in recent decades?

    a. African-American
    b. Hispanic
    c. college
    d. shoppers, or pennnysavers

19. Which area has seen the greatest decline in newspaper competition?

    a. big cities
    b. small towns
    c. suburbia
    d. rural areas

20. The biggest difference between online newspapers and their print cousins is in terms of:

    a. writing styles
    b. objectivity
    c. distribution method
    d. average reader age

CHAPTER 5: TEST ANSWER KEYS

True/False Test

01. True	05. True	09. False	13. True
02. True	06. False	10. False	14. False
03. False	07. True	11. True	15. True
04. False	08. True	12. False	

Multiple-Choice Test

01. C	06. B	11. C	16. C
02. A	07. B	12. D	17. A
03. C	08. C	13. A	18. A
04. A	09. A	14. B	19. A
05. D	10. A	15. B	20. C

-------------- **N O T E S** --------------

Chapter 6

Structure of the Magazine Industry

With this chapter we see how magazines exploit the rich potential of highly distinctive audiences. We'll examine how magazines can be organized by type and their operations by function. Then we'll look at the various roles editors perform on a magazine staff. We'll end by examining the tough and complex issues now facing this industry.

CHAPTER OBJECTIVES

.   understand the unique traits of magazines as a mass medium

.   learn one way (of many) by which magazines can be categorized

.   trace the necessary steps and job roles of getting a magazine from the drawing board to your mailbox or local store

KEY TERMS AND CONCEPTS

[ ]   general magazine characteristics (convenience, currency, editorial flexibility, ad appeal, etc.)
[ ]   estimated number of American magazines
[ ]   **magazines structured by content**, characteristics of
    [ ]   general consumer magazines
    [ ]   business publications (trade publications): [ ] vertical v [ ] horizontal
    [ ]   literary reviews and academic journals
    [ ]   newsletters
    [ ]   public relations (company) magazines
[ ]   **magazines structured by function:** [ ] production; [ ] distribution; [ ] retail
[ ]   paid circulation; [ ] controlled circulation
[ ]   online magazines; [ ] CD-ROM magazines, characteristics of both
[ ]   magazine departments: [ ] circulation: [ ] advertising ; [ ] production: [ ] editorial
[ ]   magazine lead time; [ ] dummy
[ ]   economic trends; [ ] revenue sources (subscription, single sales, and advertising)
[ ]   e-journals
[ ]   the "till-forbid" subscription policy

TOPICS FOR DISCUSSION

1. Why have publishers launched so many magazines in the last decade (some 4000)? What does that say about our society?

2. As the media continue to target highly focused audiences (a phenomenon most visible in the magazine industry), can we maintain a common ground of national cultural currency? If so, based on what media? On what content? And for whom?

3. Let's say you wanted to launch a magazine just for freshmen in your college. Itemize your audience's demographics. What advertisers might be interested? Would you go for a paid-circulation or controlled circulation basis? Why?

4. List the pros and cons of magazines as a medium, i.e., what makes them different (better or worse) than other media?

5. List the ten magazines you like most; then compare your list with several other students. Could you draw any meaningful conclusions about a person's personality simply by the list they make? Would that same list-comparison exercise work for music, TV, films, books, and so on?

6. Most editors value the editorial integrity of their magazine above all other things. "If you can't believe us," they might say, "who can you believe?" But can we believe them? How important is "reader trust" to you personally?

7. To paraphrase a popular T-shirt, "So many magazines, so little time." How do you cope with all the choices? How do you go about deciding which magazines will make the best investment in terms of your time, money, and personal or professional fulfillment?

8. Come to a class consensus on where to find the widest (or best) selection of magazines within a ten-mile radius of your campus. How far would you have to go to find foreign magazines?

9. Many editors say that a university campus is a virtual gold mine for magazine ideas (trends, experts, studies, social movements, art, music, creativity, and famous guest speakers abound). Have you ever had an idea that you thought might make a good article? How would you go about turning your idea into reality?

10. About twenty years ago there were no major magazines aimed at senior citizens; now, because of America's changing demographics, our biggest magazine (*Modern Maturity*) does just that. Zip ahead to the year 2010; what magazine (existing or yet to be) do you think will head the list?

11. Have you seen an online magazine, or seen/heard a CD-ROM magazine? What did you like or dislike about each?

Chapter 6: True/False Test

Structure of the Magazine Industry

1. Experts estimate there are about 2,500 total magazine titles currently published in the U.S.

2. Of all mass media, magazines tend to most quickly reflect our nation's changing social trends.

3. A "take-it-with-you" airline magazine is an example of a *paid-circulation* publication.

4. The trend in consumer magazines is toward smaller, highly specialized audiences.

5. Most magazines usually have long editorial preparation *lead* times.

6. A magazine "dummy" is a new magazine that didn't make it past its fourth year of publication.

7. An "e-journal" is a nickname for magazines published by and for the Generation X crowd.

8. Commercial newsletters are relatively cheap publications aimed at broad business audiences.

9. The biggest revenue source for all magazines is advertising; then subscription; then single sales.

10. You generally have to "qualify" to get a controlled-circulation magazine.

11. Magazine advertising rates are based on circulation; the higher the circulation, the more an advertiser pays for the space.

12. Publishers pay a premium to keep their magazines by supermarket checkout counters.

13. A "vertical" business publication is one that deals with all facets of a particular industry.

14. Even though there are more magazines than ever today, the magazine industry's share of national advertising has remained constant at around 21 percent over the last several years.

15. The "till-forbid subscription" idea parallels the billing procedures used by TV cable companies.

Chapter 6: Multiple Choice Test

Structure of the Magazine Industry

1. Which of the following groups is *least* likely to rely on advertising revenues?

   a. controlled-circulation magazines
   b. trade publications
   c. literary reviews and academic journals
   d. vertical publications

2. Which of these is *not* a general magazine characteristic?

   a. high pass-along readership
   b. convenience and portability
   c. attractive advertising medium
   d. best medium for quick, local coverage

3. This is the type of magazine for which you might pay $200 to $400 or more per year.

   a. trade publication
   b. commercial newsletter
   c. business publication
   d. literary review

4. *Banking Monthly* (covering the industry top to bottom) illustrates a _____ magazine.

   a. vertical
   b. horizontal
   c. commercial newsletter
   d. none of the above

5. "Till-forbid" is a magazine term that means they will:

   a. keep billing you until you tell them to stop
   b. continue sending copies at first-class rates (for speedier delivery) until you tell them otherwise
   c. provide your name to "mailing lists" unless you specifically ask them not to
   d. none of the above

6. Because of the expense involved, and lower reader interest, which of the below subjects are you least likely to see in today's magazines?

   a. investigative reporting
   b. full-color photo stories
   c. self-help pieces
   d. celebrity interviews

7. Many people, because of their particular positions, qualify to get this type of magazine free.

    a. commercial newsletter   c. controlled-circulation magazine
    b. an "e-journal"   d. horizontal publication

8. Which of these is an advantage for a general-circulation magazine?

    a. second-class postal rates   c. greater public exposure (than other magazines)
    b. added revenue (from subscriptions)   d. they enjoy *all* these advantages

9. *Security Director's Monthly* is an example of a _____ magazine.

    a. vertical   c. commercial newsletter
    b. horizontal   d. none of the above

10. A magazine *dummy* is a:

    a. graphic plan for a magazine issue   c. newspaper without advertising
    b. canceled TV show   d. free newspaper

11. In which magazine format are you most likely to hear music or see movie clips?

    a. horizontal   c. a dummy
    b. e-journal   d. CD-ROM

12. A typical consumer magazine gets about _____ percent of its revenue from advertising.

    a. 25   c. 50
    b. 50   d. variety makes figure hard to generalize

13. The two items increasing fastest in cost in today's magazine industry are:

    a. ink and rack premiums   c. paper and postage
    b. editorial and freelancers' fees   d. typesetting and printing

14. Where are you likely to get an "e-journal?"

    a. on the Internet   c. in the academic area
    b. as an employee in a big company   d. through a trade association

15. Which item below characterizes the driving trend in today's magazine industry?

a. more investigative journalism
b. subscription price wars
c. a concentration on specialized reader interests
d. new interest for online advertising outlets

16. Which of the below is *not* a general characteristic of the magazine as a mass media vehicle?

a. appeals to advertisers because of high reader identifiability
b. editorial flexibility, i.e., most magazines appeal to a wide range of people
c. relatively long editorial-preparation lead time (three to six months) from idea to publication
d. current, convenient, and relatively inexpensive

17. Online magazines have all but which of the below advantages?

a. timely: almost always "published" prior to their print cousins
b. inexpensive: you pay only for the time you're "online" with the database service
c. they take up no space and back copies are always available
d. advertisers can employ full color *and* sound with their messages

18. A magazine subscription manager generally works in the _____ department.

a. editorial
b. production
c. distribution
d. advertising

19. Which audience type is most likely to become the target of a new magazine?

a. Generation X
b. older people (45 +)
c. children
d. women

20. Where are most consumer magazines sold?

a. supermarkets
b. drugstores
c. bookstores
d. newsstands

CHAPTER 6: TEST ANSWER KEYS

True/False Test

01. False	05. True	09. False	13. True
02. True	06. False	10. True	14. True
03. True	07. False	11. True	15. True
04. True	08. False	12. True	

Multiple-Choice Test

01. C	06. A	11. D	16. B
02. D	07. C	12. D	17. D
03. B	08. C	13. C	18. C
04. A	09. B	14. A	19. B
05. A	10. A	15. C	20. A

-------------- **N O T E S** --------------

Chapter 7

Structure of the Book Industry

This chapter focuses on book publishing's pragmatic side (structure, methods, and economics) along with its more subjective side--the real contributions provided by books to our culture and society.

CHAPTER OBJECTIVES

. determine the unique characteristics of books as a mass medium

. view the industry as organized by function and its products by type

. follow a book's development from idea to store shelf

KEY TERMS AND CONCEPTS

[ ] characteristics of the book as a unique mass medium
[ ] book industry organization: [ ] publishers; [ ] distributors; [ ] retailers
[ ] books by type:

[ ] trade	[ ] university presses
[ ] religious	[ ] elementary and secondary textbooks
[ ] professional	[ ] college text
[ ] book clubs	[ ] standardized tests
[ ] mail-order	[ ] subscription reference books
[ ] mass market paperbacks	[ ] audiovisual and other media

[ ] ownership trends (two major)
[ ] major departments of a publishing firm (major responsibilities)

[ ] editorial	[ ] marketing
[ ] production	[ ] general administration or business

[ ] the main sources for book ideas: [ ] agents; [ ] unsolicited sources; [ ] editor-generated
[ ] *stitch* vs. *perfect* book binding methods
[ ] digital books (CD-ROM); [ ] books "online," trends
[ ] economic trends of the book industry
[ ] symbiotic relationship of books to other media
[ ] the major issues facing the book industry today

TOPICS FOR DISCUSSION

1. Although we're publishing more books than ever before, fewer of us (proportionately) are reading them. Should we be concerned?

2. List ten books that *significantly* altered world history; tell how, why, and when. Since the U.S. represents only a fraction of the world's population, why are so many of the books on your list written by American authors?

3. List ten books (from all cultures, nations, and historical epochs) that represent the best works of all time (fiction or non-fiction); this may sound similar to Question 2, but the results should be quite different. Justify your choices.

4. Do you see any danger in an increasing foreign ownership of American publishing firms?

5. Recently someone published a comic book depicting how mass murderer and cannibal Jeffrey Dahmer committed his crimes. Families of the victims were outraged; the artist replied that he had a right to make a buck. Your views?

6. Can censorship ever be justified? Is there any subject, theme, or content so overwhelmingly detrimental to society that we shouldn't allow its publication?

7. *Brother Eagle, Sister Sky* is a recent award-winning children's book. In it, an ecological message attributed to Chief Seattle (circa 1850s) was found later--after the book was a success--to have actually been written by a 1970s Hollywood screenwriter. The publisher refused to change the attribution, saying that it was the message that mattered, not the author. Do you agree?

8. No one in the U.S. censors books with a "censored" stamp, but that doesn't mean books can't be censored in other ways. A book store that refuses to carry a book, in effect, censors it; a school that "elects" not to buy a book, in effect, censors it; a library that removes a book over a patron's protest, in effect, becomes a censor. Are there other methods of censorship? Have you ever suspected any efforts to censor books in any institution in your home area?

9. The U.S. literacy rate ranks among the lowest of technological nations. Why? Does it matter?

10. The astronomer Carl Sagan once said that the trick was "not how many books you read, but which ones." How do *you* decide which books to read?

11. Someone offers you a dream job--with one hitch. "Before we hire you," your employer says, "let me measure your range of interests by the books you've voluntarily read in the past two years." What books will your list contain?

12. Have you ever bought or listened to a "book" on tape? What were your impressions? Are they time savers? What are the essential differences between them and their print cousins?

Chapter 7: True/False Test

Structure of the Book Industry

1. Most book publishers are "generalists," i.e., they do not specialize in a one-subject area.

2. Relative to the overall population, books are read by a comparably small audience.

3. College textbooks are typically produced, for the public good, on a break-even-plus-one-percent-profit basis, most of their customers being libraries and students.

4. The book industry is the only mass medium that doesn't use distribution middlemen, i.e., books are generally shipped directly from the publisher to bookstores or other retail outlets.

5. Unlike other media, book publishers perform careful pre-publishing analyses of their products so that they can accurately predict how well the material is likely to do with the public.

6. Books are the most *mass* of the mass media, a best seller easily selling over 100 million copies.

7. The two chief trends in book industry ownership today are: (a) increasing foreign ownership, and (b) consolidation (company mergers).

8. The marketing department of a book publisher is ultimately responsible for accepting or rejecting a book for publication.

9. Most trade books (popular press) are submitted to the publisher through literary agents.

10. One reason that CD-ROM books have yet to become popular is because of the inability of the publisher to include photographs or artwork on the CD, as they can with a paper medium.

11. The way your text is held together is exemplifies the saddle-stitch, or sewing machine, method.

12. The chief difference between *a mail order publication house* and a *book club* is that the former both produces *and* markets its books via direct mail with "no-membership-obligation" terms.

13. Largely due to declining readership, book industry profits continue to slide slowly downward.

14. The now-abandoned *books-on-tape* format was a short-lived and hugely unprofitable venture.

15. Book publishing is an isolated medium; books rarely interact with, or depend upon, other media.

Chapter 7: Multiple-Choice Test

Structure of the Book Industry

1. Which of the following is *not* an accurate reflection of the book as a mass medium?

   a. to be considered a best seller, a book must sell *at least* 20 million copies nationwide
   b. books are the *least* "mass" of the mass media
   c. some books have an enormous cultural impact yet sell to only a fraction of our population
   d. both fiction and non-fiction books can enjoy subsidiary profits (films, TV spinoffs, and so on)

2. What book type is, by far, the number one leader in book sales:

   a. elementary and high school texts   c. mass market paperbacks
   b. religious   d. trade (popular press)

3. U.S. publishers introduce about _____ new book titles each year.

   a. 10,000   c. 50,000
   b. 25,000   d. 75,000

4. Who would an aspiring author most likely need in order to break into the publishing world?

   a. an agent   c. an editor
   b. a publisher   d. a book critic or reviewer

5. Which of these published items are you *most* likely to find in a consumer book store?

   a. professional publications   c. secondary textbooks
   b. trade books (popular press)   d. audiovisual and other media

6. Which book publishing department would generally be in charge of trying to get an author on a TV show to help promote his or her book?

   a. editorial   c. marketing
   b. production   d. administration

7. The major book publishing trend of the 1990s:

    a. more foreign investors   c. *a* and *b*
    b. more firms being consolidated   d. none of the above

8. Publishers get most of their book ideas from three of these sources; which doesn't belong?

    a. agent recommendations   c. recognized authors
    b. readers   d. suggestions from editors

9. The _____ department normally decides a book's physical features, such as type style, page size, paper, printing method, binding, and so on.

    a. editorial   c. marketing
    b. production   d. business

10. The most recent symbiotic media partner the book industry has found is:

    a. the film industry   c. television infomercials
    b. newspapers and magazines d. talk radio

11. Identify the item that is *not* one of the emerging trends in bookstores today:

    a. a switch to smaller, more specialized shops
    b. a switch to the "superstore," a larger, more generalized outlet
    c. inclusion of material other than print, e.g., CD-ROMs, audio tapes, games, and software
    d. an atmosphere conducive to browsing, including lounge chairs, soft music, and coffee or tea

12. Publishers get *most* of their profits from:

    a. original book sales   c. paperback reprint rights
    b. foreign reprint rights   d. subsidies from film-rights sales

13. Find the false statement about mass market paperbacks.

    a. most are sold in retail outlets other than bookstores
    b. they are on the low end (seven percent) of book industry sales volume
    c. topics include both fiction and non-fiction
    d. they are the only book type distributed *directly* to retail outlets from the publisher

14. *Slush* book manuscripts are:

    a. books with more graphics than words   c. unsolicited books
    b. foreign reprints   d. update editions of proven best sellers

15. Digital books on CD-ROM can offer:

    a. the complete book text   c. music or speech clips
    b. video or photo clips   d. all the above

16. What age group buys the most books?

    a. 5 - 10   c. 35 - 49
    b. 15 - 20   d. 55 - 75

17. With what book department is the author most likely to communicate?

    a. marketing   c. business
    b. production   d. editorial

18. Responsibility for the publicity or promotion of a book falls to which department?

    a. marketing   c. business
    b. production   d. editorial

19. In what area are you likely to find the most interactivity between reader and publisher?

    a. retail superstores   c. CD-ROM books
    b. online outlets   d. author-autograph sessions

20. Three of these items do not really concern book industry critics; which issue *does* concern them?

    a. today's authors can't write nearly as well as writers just a few decades ago
    b. corporate mergers tend to emphasize bottom-line profits over a book's content quality
    c. books-on-tape are cutting into the sales of legitimate books
    d. CD-ROMs and online publishing have no place in the book publishing industry

CHAPTER 7:   TEST ANSWER KEYS

True/False Test

01. False	05. False	09. True	13. False
02. True	06. False	10. False	14. False
03. False	07. True	11. False	15. False
04. False	08. False	12. True	

Multiple-Choice Test

01. A	06. C	11. A	16. C
02. D	07. C	12. A	17. D
03. C	08. B	13. D	18. A
04. A	09. B	14. C	19. B
05. B	10. C	15. D	20. B

------------- **N O T E S** -------------

Chapter 8

History of Radio and Recording

This is the story of how two mediums--recording and radio--have shared a seventy-year roller-coaster ride of technical and social development. It includes a cast of often eccentric players, among them, inventors, the U.S. Navy, criminals, some of America's biggest businesses, rappers, band leaders, and DJs. You'll see how legal battles, business mergers, greed, technical problems, wars, a depression, and the Supreme Court somehow managed to give us the two mediums we take so much for granted today: radio and the recording industry.

CHAPTER OBJECTIVES

• trace the technological, economic and social history of the radio and recording industries

KEY TERMS AND CONCEPTS

[ ] Thomas Edison's 1877 cylinder-based phonograph; [ ] Emile Berliner's "gramophone"
[ ] Guglielmo Marconi's 1896 "wireless" (using Morse code to send messages)
[ ] Lee De Forest and his vacuum tube, significance of
[ ] nickelodeons (recording); [ ] Victrola, 1906
[ ] KDKA and the Conrad-Horne-Westinghouse story (1920)
[ ] factors that made radio a mass medium (audience size, mass production, home uses)
[ ] AT&T's "advertising solution" to the radio revenue problem (WEAF, 1922); [ ] premiums
[ ] networking (how and why it was a profit-making idea)
[ ] NBC Red and Blue networks, 1926 (twenty-eight affiliates); CBS, 1927 (thirteen affiliates)
[ ] Radio Act of 1927 (FRC, Federal Radio Commission), reasons for and achievements of
[ ] juke box's 1930s role in saving recording industry
[ ] Federal Communication Commission (FCC), 1934, significance of
[ ] radio programming content and trends (reasons for them) 1930s - 1940s
[ ] genesis of the American Broadcasting Company (ABC) in 1943
[ ] three main reasons why FM had a hard time taking off after WW II
[ ] effects TV had on radio (network drop plus new reliance on records and local advertisers)
[ ] "Battle of the Speeds"; [ ] emergence of small record labels and radio as a promotional device
[ ] format radio, purpose and types, e.g., MOR, CW, new age, rock, Top 40, talk, news, rap, etc.
[ ] DJs; [ ] payola; [ ] clock hour; [ ] DAB and DAT, likely effects on the sound industries
[ ] Nonduplication Rule, 1965 (a.k.a. 50-50 Rule)
[ ] the FCC's "duopolies" ruling: purpose, restrictions, and effects (the 20/20 and 2/2 rules)
[ ] CDS, MTV, and music videos: reasons for the effects they've had on the recording industry
[ ] major music content trends, 1945 to present

TOPICS FOR DISCUSSION

1. Everybody knows that music stores play music in the background, but few know that record companies often pay for the privilege with either cash or free recordings. The idea, of course, is that if you hear it, you'll buy it. Is this just another form of payola?

2. Now that they're available, would you recommend buying a DAT player? Why or why not?

3. Did the recording industry ultimately fragment radio, or did radio fragment the music industry? Or did *we* do it to both of them?

4. Can you outline your own personal history in terms of music tastes? Has it changed? If so, how, and how often? Do those changes--if any--parallel your changes in your favorite radio station?

5. Are the radio and recording industries over-reacting to the perceived "threat" of DAT?

6. The FCC exercises regulatory control over the entire electromagnetic spectrum; any device that operates in or interferes with those wavelengths comes under its jurisdiction. Radio and TV are easy examples; others include computers, microwaves, telephones, CB, and walkie-talkies. Can you name other examples?

7. Why haven't we, unlike the rest of the world, ever responded warmly to shortwave radio sets?

8. Although ragtime, jazz, folk, R&B, classical, and musicals are still around (and still influence today's music), their day in the sun has passed. Will rock ever face the same fate?

9. Almost every radio station's call letters have a history behind them, i.e., they're usually acronyms for someone, some company, or some organization (generally long forgotten). What do the call letters of your favorite station stand for?

10. Estimate the total dollar investment you've made in both sound equipment and recordings (and please include any music videos). How long do you think your recordings are "good for"--not how long will they last, but rather how long do you think your *interest* in those sounds will last?

11. Will you be willing to give up your receiver and tape player in order to switch over to the much higher priced DAB and DAT formats? What about buying an AM stereo receiver for your car?

12. Nickelodeons, or more precisely quarterlodeons, may be making a comeback. At the 1992 electronics consumer show, several companies hawked pay-as-you-listen devices to mount atop radios, telephones, tape players, etc. Aimed at parents, the companies called it a good way to teach teenagers such things as savings habits and moderating leisure time activities (not to mention helping to pay the electric and phone bills). Reactions?

Chapter 8: True/False Test

History of Radio and Recording

1. Ironically, it was the phone company--AT&T--that came up with the idea of charging businesses a fee for radio time, thus beginning the idea of broadcast advertising.

2. Nationwide, AM radio still has far more listeners than FM.

3. KDKA, in 1920, was the first official radio station (and it's now the oldest.)

4. A *clock hour* is a radio rating technique similar to Nielsen's TV ratings system.

5. NBC's "Red" network became the MBS radio network.

6. Marconi became the first person to profit from ship-to-ship wireless communications.

7. DAB will make sound quality differences between AM and FM essentially nonexistent.

8. The FCC's Nonduplication Rule makes it illegal for an AM station to broadcast more than 50 percent of its programming content on a sister FM station.

9. In the 1930s, the Great Depression nearly forced radio out of business, while the recording industry's profits flourished (largely due to the introduction of the Victrola).

10. The predominant type of content a radio station broadcasts is called its *format*.

11. Radio stations are increasingly looking for larger audiences with a variety of music tastes.

12. The Battle of the Speeds refers to the sound quality differences between records, tape, and CDs.

13. Lee De Forest invented Morse Code, thus making communications possible on the "wireless."

14. TV forced radio stations to find new programming formats and new revenue sources.

15. Payola, once an illegal practice, is now simply considered a common promotional technique.

Chapter 8: Multiple-Choice Test

History of Radio and Recording

1. The original name of radio was:

   a. radiography
   b. wireless

   c. radiotelegraphy
   d. hertz

2. On which of the below could you hear radio signals without the benefit of electricity?

   a. juke boxes
   b. nickelodeon

   c. a crystal set
   d. the Victrola

3. After a 1943 Supreme Court anti-monopoly ruling, ABC was formed from which network?

   a. NBC
   b. CBS

   c. MBS
   d. none of the above

4. What device helped revive the recording industry in the 1930s?

   a. the Victrola
   b. the 45 rpm format

   c. juke box
   d. radio

5. His idea of a flat-disk recording medium (the gramophone) eventually won out.

   a. Thomas Edison
   b. Guglielmo Marconi

   c. Emile Berliner
   d. Lee De Forest

6. Thomas Edison thought his "phonograph" would be used:

   a. for music playback, pretty much the way it is (or was)
   b. as a device to record the dying words of famous personalities
   c. in the business office, as a dictation aid
   d. by schools, as an educational tool

7. He invented the vacuum tube.

   a. Thomas Edison
   b. Guglielmo Marconi

   c. Emile Berliner
   d. Lee De Forest

8. Early TV triggered drastic changes in radio's environment. Which of these wasn't one of them?

   a. all network affiliations ended
   b. many programs switched to TV

   c. national ad revenue began drying up
   d. over 40 percent of radio stations folded

9. Before radio could become a mass medium, it needed all but which of the below items?

   a. a mass audience
   b. mass produced receivers

   c. high quality programming
   d. reasonably reliable revenue sources

10. In 1934, President Franklin Roosevelt finally brought tighter control over the entire broadcasting industry when he inaugurated the:

    a. Federal Radio Commission
    b. Federal Communications Commission

    c. Maritime Radio Act
    d. Telecommunications Commission Act

11. Especially in city markets, FM radio has largely forced AM radio to drastically alter its formats; which of these formats has AM radio largely since avoided?

    a. talk radio
    b. Top 40

    c. news
    d. specialty content (e.g., business and religion)

12. Congress instituted the Radio Act of 1927 primarily in order to:

    a. bring order to radio station frequencies and transmission power
    b. make networks possible
    c. get the U.S. Navy out of the job of regulating radio
    d. regulate broadcast advertising

13. The primary purpose for a radio station to create a particular format is to:

    a. enable them to hire an expert staff for a given music genre
    b. attract a highly identifiable audience in order to attract a particular group of advertisers
    c. avoid the expense of buying a wide variety of programming materials
    d. conform to FCC licensing regulations

14. They were radio's "slowest" program format:

    a. adventure series
    b. news reports
    c. baseball broadcasts
    d. soap operas

15. Relative to today's prices, early radio sets in the 1920s were:

    a. about the same
    b. much more expensive
    c. much less expensive

16. Which of the below wasn't a reason FM had a hard time getting started?

    a. it began about the same time as television
    b. its original frequencies were reassigned, thus making the all the prototype receivers obsolete
    c. Some AM stations bought FM stations and broadcast identical content, making would-be FM buyers wonder, "Why bother?"
    d. FM reception was originally much worse than AM

17. The FCC's "duopolies" regulation states that a corporation may now own:

    a. no more than 50 radio stations
    b. any number of AM stations *or* FM stations, but *not* a mixture of both types
    c. no more than two AM and two FM stations
    d. no more than 20 AM *and* 20 FM, *and* no more than two of each in the same market area

18. The newest promotional aid for the recording industry is/are:

    a. DAB and DATs
    b. CDs
    c. MTV and similar networks
    d. FCC

19. The most popular radio format (before music) and also the last to fade from network radio were the _____ programs.

    a. action-adventure
    b. live music
    c. comedy
    d. soap operas

20. The principle reason to be part of a network is to:

    a. share programming costs
    b. gain prestige
    c. merge with a larger parent company
    d. get better access to the recording industry

CHAPTER 8: TEST ANSWER KEYS

True/False Test

01. True	05. False	09. False	13. False
02. False	06. True	10. True	14. True
03. True	07. True	11. False	15. False
04. False	08. True	12. False	

Multiple-Choice Test

01. B	06. C	11. B	16. D
02. C	07. D	12. A	17. D
03. A	08. D	13. B	18. C
04. C	09. C	14. D	19. D
05. C	10. B	15. B	20. A

-------------- **N O T E S** --------------

Chapter 9

Structure of the Radio Industry

This chapter examines the radio industry as an increasingly competitive, fragmented, consolidated, and profit-savvy medium. We'll see how competition, technology, new FCC regulations, and an ever-changing audience have helped make this industry mass media's reigning chameleon.

CHAPTER OBJECTIVES

. study the radio industry's current trends in format, ownership, technology, and its role as a unique mass medium

. learn operational differences between station types and job roles

. examine current issues in audience promotions, talk radio's new power, and the impact of shrinking audience markets and increasing competition for advertising revenue

KEY TERMS AND CONCEPTS

[ ] characteristics of radio as a mass medium; [ ] duopolies: pros and cons
[ ] average number of radios per person (2); [ ] per household (6); [ ] weekly listening hours (25)
[ ] number of stations (11,500, and growing)
[ ] purpose of radio syndicates and networks
[ ] AM (amplitude modulation), characteristics of; [ ] AM channels: clear, regional, and local
[ ] FM (frequency modulation), characteristics of
[ ] format, three basic types: music, ethnic, and news/talk; [ ] radio's two prime-time times
[ ] format/market homogenization trends, reasons for
[ ] advantages of a station being "on the bird"
[ ] top management positions: general manager and program director, responsibilities of
[ ] radio departments: sales, news, programming, and engineering
[ ] format wheel (format clock or clock hour); [ ] cycle (period before program order repeats)
[ ] call-in "delay system" and the telephone screener, reasons for
[ ] rate card; [ ] radio revenue sources: national; national spot; local
[ ] ASCAP and BMI music licensors: functions they perform for both stations and copyright owners
[ ] noncommercial radio, characteristics of and support systems for
[ ] National Public Radio (NPR); [ ] Public Radio International (PRI)
[ ] station promotions, reasons for
[ ] issues: talk-shows' growing political power; ignored under 18 and over 55 age markets
[ ] Digital Audio Broadcasting (DAB) and [ ] Radio Data System (RDS), characteristics of

TOPICS FOR DISCUSSION

1. A key FCC operational guideline is that broadcasters must serve the public interest. Although stations may do that individually, what do we do when they collectively ignore age-minority markets simply because those people don't have big buying power?

2. Given the Constitution's guarantee of free speech, should the FCC fine stations for language, music, or topics it thinks is inappropriate? How far is too far? Based on whose standards?

3. What regulatory differences separate print and broadcast media?

4. Should DJs be licensed by the FCC?

5. Is DAB worth the enormous costs involved--to both the consumer and the industry? Who stands to gain what? Same question, but this time about a Radio Data System (RDS).

6. If your college started a new (or another) radio station, consider for a moment who the audience might be. Would it make a difference if you were a dormitory or a commuter-based college? Why or how? Make a list of potential audiences and a programming format that might attract them.. Then make a list of advertisers who might be interested in reaching those people.

7. Try a quick class survey of favorite stations and formats; do the results agree with your text's demographic presumptions?

8. Defenders of what others might call pornographic magazines usually defend the magazines with an argument such as, "If you don't want to see the pictures, then don't buy the magazine." Might you use a similar argument to defend racy radio by saying, "Hey, if it offends you, don't listen." Is there a qualitative difference between the two situations?

9. Can you name the nearest clear-channel AM station? The nearest station to have NPR or PRI programming? An ethnic station? A shock-jock station? One with sex-oriented programs?

10. How many hours a week do you personally estimate you listen to radio? How much do you use radio passively (for background purposes)? What about actively, that is, situations in which you must listen closely to what's going on? Can you honestly study with music in the background?

11. List the top three things you think would improve your favorite radio station.

12. Have you ever won any promotions from a station, e.g., money, tickets, or trips? Explain.

13. Have you ever phoned into a talk radio station and expressed your views on the air. Discuss.

Chapter 9:   True/False Test

Structure of the Radio Industry

1. FM waves bounce off the ionosphere while AM waves travel in a straight line (much like TV).

2. A radio station, like the newspaper, is essentially a local medium.

3. FM listenership beats AM by about a 3:1 ratio.

4. AM signals, because they're stronger, are less likely than FM signals to be affected by outside electrical interference.

5. A "regional" channel radio station is designed to broadcast farther than a "clear" channel station.

6. Thunderstorms cause more interference with an AM receiver than an FM because the AM waves are closer to the electrical energy wavelengths on the electromagnetic spectrum than FM.

7. Only one major area in radio hasn't changed since 1952; there are still only four radio networks.

8. The two prime times for radio are between 10-2 P.M. and 6-8 P.M.

9. Radio talk shows, particularly ones dealing with current events, tend to support a politically conservative viewpoint.

10. Most people listen to radio about twenty-five hours a week.

11. The number of radio stations in the U.S. has declined considerably in the past 25 years.

12. Publicity activities geared to attract more listeners to a station are called *promotions*.

13. Most noncommercial radio stations are owned by public relations companies.

14. The number of radios in the U.S. average about two per person and six per household.

15. The general manager is a radio station's top management official.

Chapter 9: Multiple Choice Test

Structure of the Radio Industry

1. Which AM channel type is best heard farthest away from a station?

    a. clear
    b. regional

    c. local
    d. duopoly

2. Radio syndicates and networks are now essentially alike, their primary purpose being to:

    a. provide stations with prepaid national advertising spots
    b. generate the transmitting power necessary for a "clear channel" broadcast
    c. supply prepackaged programming formats of all kinds
    d. modulate AM and FM frequencies

3. Some stations across the country may have an almost identical "sound." This is otherwise known as:

    a. duopolization
    b. format homogenization

    c. format cycling
    d. being "on the bird"

4. Generally the most complex and expensive radio format to run is:

    a. music
    b. talk

    c. all news
    d. ethnic

5. Which of these isn't an advantage of DAB over today's analog broadcasting system?

    a. better audio quality
    b. computer-like interfacing

    c. cheaper to transmit
    d. travels ten times as far as an AM signal

6. Which is *not* a typical radio department:

    a. sales
    b. editorial

    c. programming
    d. engineering

7. A _____ is essentially a schedule of what a station will broadcast in a sixty-minute period.

   a. frequency modulation
   b. format wheel

   c. Radio Data System (RDS)
   d. cycle

8. Find the false statement about today's radio industry:

   a. there are approximately 125 million radio sets in the U.S.
   b. station mergers and buy outs are increasing
   c. local advertising makes up the biggest source of revenue
   d. you can't own more than two AM and two FM stations in the same market area

9. The two most popular formats on radio today (as measured by ratings) are:

   a. talk and news
   b. middle of the road and new age

   c. adult contemporary and country western
   d. urban contemporary and album-oriented rock

10. What format is coming under increasing scrutiny for the political clout it seems to wield?

    a. National Public Radio
    b. news

    c. talk
    d. Public Radio International

11. There are about _____ radio stations in the U.S. today.

    a. 750
    b. 3500

    c. 11,500
    d. 24,500

12. Being "on the bird" means your station is getting:

    a. payola
    b. reviewed by the FCC

    c. technical assistance
    d. canned programming from a satellite system

13. Which of the below is a *primary* reason for forming a duopoly?

    a. format homogenization
    b. cutting costs through consolidations

    c. qualify for "clear channel" status
    d. get ASCAP and BMI rate reductions

14. A Radio Data System (RDS) receiver would most function like a:

   a. computerized radio and printer
   b. shortwave radio set
   c. powerful stereo system
   d. cordless telephone

15. Most stations shy away from the under 18 and over 55 crowds because:

   a. they don't constitute a significantly sizeable audience
   b. neither group has enough buying power to attract advertisers
   c. surveys show neither group likes radio very much
   d. one group is too young and the other too old for today's music

16. Radio talk show hosts are protected from crank callers by:

   a. FCC regulation
   b. amplitude modulation
   c. delay devices and phone screeners
   d. the station's engineering staff

17. ASCAP and BMI permit stations to play:

   a. songs on a pay-per-play basis
   b. whatever they want for a predetermined fee
   c. only officially sanctioned ASCAP or BMI recordings
   d. anything, just as long as the DJ mentions both the recording artist *and* the song title

18. Which of the below is not a *major* format group?

   a. urban contemporary (UC)
   b. talk/news
   c. ethnic
   d. music

19. Which of these isn't a type of radio advertising?

   a. national
   b. national spot (regional)
   c. local
   d. cycled

20. What you pay for advertising time depends primarily on a station's:

   a. market share
   b. channel strength
   c. format
   d. clock hour rate

CHAPTER 9: TEST ANSWER KEYS

True/False Test

01. False	05. False	09. True	13. False
02. True	06. True	10. True	14. True
03. True	07. False	11. False	15. True
04. False	08. False	12. True	

Multiple-Choice Test

01. A	06. B	11. C	16. C
02. C	07. B	12. D	17. B
03. B	08. A	13. B	18. A
04. C	09. C	14. A	19. D
05. D	10. C	15. B	20. A

-------------- N O T E S --------------

Chapter 10

Structure of the Recording Industry

This chapter takes us on a tour of mass media's smallest medium, but one that exerts considerable influence beyond its size. We'll see how the industry organizes itself (talent, production, distribution, and retail); in addition, we'll study the roles and responsibilities of the people in a typical recording company. Next, we'll see how new technology is completely revamping how music is played and recorded; next we'll explore how much profit the industry and the individuals in it are likely to make.

CHAPTER OBJECTIVES

. learn how the music industry is organized and how its various departments function

. analyze industry trends in technology, economics, and ownership

. explore a few of the social issues now facing the music industry

KEY TERMS AND CONCEPTS

[ ] industry characteristics (ownership, volatility, economics, business, and talent)
[ ] industry organization:
    [ ] talent
    [ ] production
    [ ] distribution
    [ ] retail
[ ] distribution modes: [ ] direct retail; [ ] rack jobbers; [ ] one-stops; [ ] direct consumer sales
[ ] major departments of a recording company, responsibilities of
    [ ] artists and repertoire (A&R)
    [ ] sales and distribution
    [ ] advertising and merchandising
    [ ] business
    [ ] promotion
    [ ] publicity
    [ ] artist development
[ ] demo; [ ] back masking
[ ] approximate number of singles and albums released in U.S. annually
[ ] performers: odds of "making it" (about 1500 to 1)
[ ] current issues: selective activism; gangsta rap
[ ] DATs: problems, promises, and restrictions

TOPICS FOR DISCUSSION

1. What are the pros and cons of foreign companies owning five of the six major U.S. record companies ?

2. Is back masking really a serious issue? Regardless of an artist's original intent, do you think the messages are ever affective?

3. Should any lyrics, regardless of language used or topic, ever be censored by government so as to prohibit a song's sale, live performance, or airing over radio? (Remember 2 Live Crew's *As Nasty as They Wanna Be*.)

4. Do warning labels on records work? Are they any more effective, or useful, than movie ratings?

5. How long will rock music dominate the industry (now at over 60 percent of sales)? Do you see other mainstream candidates?

6. Because of the industry's move toward consolidation, a conservative profit-making approach is sure to follow; can music survive "the establishment?" Or *is* music the establishment?

7. Almost all of us have been in, worked with, or know someone in, a "garage band." Share your most memorable stories.

8. An emerging issue in the film business is the potential use of "compu-thespians," actors who aren't human beings but rather a computer-animated fabrication. "Foul!" cry actors. But what about today's music groups--is their music really theirs, or is it also a product of computers, synthesizers, and multitrack recording studios? Or does it matter?

9. Political protest folk music was a common fare during the late 1960s, much of it having a big impact on how people felt about war, government, and the establishment. Is music an appropriate soap box for social or political protest? Other than "rappers," are there any groups that do it today? Do we really listen to those lyrics or are we just drumming to their beat?

10. Do you favor adopting warning codes, similar to what films use, for use on CDS or tapes?

11. Describe the changes you've seen in music stores in your life; list the additions and deletions in merchandise. What are the changes, if any, in service? Are all the changes improvements?

12. With so little competition among music makers, what do you think the chances are for price fixing? Should music profits be somehow regulated by the government?

13. Some critics worry that the music industry may stagnate if record companies stay conservative and don't risk looking for a "new sound." Have you heard any "new sound" that might qualify for the next generation of music evolution?

Chapter 10: True/False Test

Structure of the Recording Industry

1. A surprising turn in the music industry is a recent trend towards retail fragmentation, with many innovative smaller stores outselling the record "superstores" and therefore growing in popularity and numbers.

2. Of the six top recording firms, only one is American owned.

3. In the music industry, *A&R* stands for arranger and recorder.

4. The record rack jobber would typically service stores such as K-Mart, Sears, Wal-Mart, J.C. Penny's, and so on.

5. The *"one-stop"* distributor would typically distribute records to jukebox operators and small, independent retail outlets.

6. The U.S. exports far more discs and tapes than it imports.

7. It's nearly "a must" today to release a music video along with a newly released album or single.

8. The best way to get a studio to listen to a demo is to send it to their publicity department.

9. Analog technology is mechanically reproduced sound or images; digital technology is computer-based, using 0s and 1s to record and playback. Analog masters wear out; digital masters don't.

10. The chief drawback of digital audio tape (DAT) is that, like CDs, you can't erase and rerecord music on them.

11. With multitrack recording, a group doesn't even have to be together to record a song.

12. Of all mass media, the recording industry employs the fewest people (not counting performers).

13. Congress has recently placed a ban on selling "gangsta rap" in retail stores.

14. The two main income sources for recording stars today are record and book royalties.

15. The odds of a new recording group making the big time is about 50,000 to 1.

Chapter 10: Multiple Choice Test

Structure of the Recording Industry

1. _____ music accounts for about 60 percent of the record industry's total annual sales.

   a. Country/western   c. New age
   b. Rock   d. R&B and jazz

2. Of the four major music distribution systems, the _____ method is easily the most influential, accounting for about 60 percent of sales.

   a. direct-retail   c. rack jobber
   b. one-stop   d. direct-consumer

3. Which of the firms listed below is the only remaining U.S. record firm?

   a. Time Warner, Inc.   c. RCA
   b. Sony Records   d. MCA

4. Who are the talent scouts in the record industry?

   a. A&R staff   c. promotion
   b. publicity   d. artist development

5. What technological development made it possible for a group to record song parts individually and later merge them into a finished cut?

   a. multitrack recording   c. "Indies"
   b. synthesizers   d. computerized music databases

6. The music industry has now gone entirely to _____ technology.

   a. analog   c. laser
   b. digital   d. microwave

7. Step One for a new group, in order to get produced and signed, is to put together a:

    a. road-tour
    b. demo tape

    c. concert tour
    d. new sound

8. The advantage of digital over analog recording technology is:

    a. digital master never wears out
    b. digital recordings can be edited

    c. that it makes multitrack recordings possible
    d. all the above

9. Which pair of music departments works *most* closely with one another?

    a. A&R and business
    b. advertising and promotion

    c. sales/distribution and publicity
    d. business and artist development

10. In the recording industry, covert satanic references are usually associated with:

    a. lip-synching
    b. digital synthesizing

    c. back masking
    d. *laying down* tracks

11. About how many singles and albums are released annually in the U.S.?

    a. 5000 and 2500
    b. 8000 and 4000

    c. 10000 and 5000
    d. 15000 and 7500

12. What record department generally works as an intermediary between an artist and the press?

    a. A&R
    b. advertising

    c. promotion
    d. publicity

13. When finished, a studio-produced multitrack tape must eventually be reduced to a _____ track version for commercial release.

    a. 2
    b. 4

    c. 6
    d. 8

14. One of the most influential outlets for a new release to get national exposure is through:

    a. a late-night TV show, e.g., *Letterman*
    b. MTV spots

    c. a network specializing in alternative music
    d. a big-city MOR-format radio station

15. The typical method of payment for a new music group is:

    a. on a when-we-get-it (sales), you-get-it (royalties) basis
    b. a one-year, set-salary contract
    c. cash advanced against future profits
    d. according to standard rates set by ASCAP

16. Which of the below is *not* currently true of the music industry?

    a. *ownership:* dominated by small-to-medium independent labels
    b. *talent:* dominated by a few multimillion dollar groups and single artists
    c. *distribution:* dominated by rackjobbers
    d. *economics:* dominated by roller-coaster trends, currently going up

17. The CD has virtually caused the extinction of:

    a. cassette tapes   c. DAT
    b. vinyl records   d. Sony Walkmans

18. After recording sales, a music group's second biggest source of revenue is most likely to be:

    a. book royalties   c. composer royalties
    b. personal appearances   d. radio royalties

19. While many record groups have helped raise tremendous amounts of money by giving concerts for various charitable causes, many critics worry that:

    a. the money never gets to where it should
    b. many fans, after paying their money, may assume the crisis has been solved
    c. the groups are performing more for publicity's sake than for charity's
    d. too much of the revenue goes to "expenses," leaving little net revenue for the actual cause

20. DAT technology really arrived years ago; it was temporarily blocked, however, because of concerns that people might use DATs to make illegal, CD-quality tapes from other sources. Congress broke the deadlock by ruling that:

    a. CD players and DAT recorders be made incompatible
    b. the revenue loss due to piracy didn't outweigh the public good of restraining DAT technology
    c. DAT players insert a high-pitch noise whenever they record anything off a CD-ROM
    d. a surcharge be put on the sale of DAT players and tapes to compensate for pirating

CHAPTER 10: TEST ANSWER KEYS

True/False Test

01. False	05. True	09. True	13. False
02. True	06. True	10. False	14. False
03. False	07. True	11. True	15. False
04. True	08. False	12. True	

Multiple-Choice Test

01. B	06. B	11. A	16. A
02. C	07. B	12. D	17. B
03. A	08. D	13. A	18. B
04. A	09. B	14. B	19. B
05. A	10. C	15. C	20. D

-------------- N O T E S --------------

Chapter 11

History of Film and Television

This chapter tells the fascinating story of the intertwining history and rivalry of two superficially diverse but now essentially interdependent media: film and television. We'll look back at film's early experiments and excesses and follow through the golden years of Hollywood--the studios, stars, and superhits. As a new entertainment force debuted--television--we'll see how each medium looked at one another first as rivals and later as inseparable partners. Our study takes us through the various content themes of both mediums, suggesting why one topic was suited for one generation only to be discarded by the next.

CHAPTER OBJECTIVES

.   trace the technological and economic evolution of the film and TV industries; see how audience reactions helped shape both

.   understand the contributing social influences of film and TV and how the two diverse media eventually became so co-dependent

KEY TERMS AND CONCEPTS

[ ] Vitascope (projector, Thomas Edison); [ ] Kinetoscope (camera, William Dickson)
[ ] Early movie history highlights
[ ] phi phenomenon; [ ] persistence of vision
[ ] nickelodeons (contributions to film development)
[ ] Motion Picture Patents Company (MPPC): who, why, and what they were
[ ] film industry's three major components: [ ] production; [ ] distribution; [ ] exhibition
[ ] star system
[ ] Film industry's consolidation and growth, highlights
[ ] block booking (what is was, why it happened)
[ ] formula films, reasons for and constituent elements of; [ ] double features
[ ] the "Studio Years," 1930 to 1950, Hollywood's Golden Era, characteristics of
[ ] Television: the Advent of Competition and Change, highlights
[ ] videotape, the importance of this development to TV
[ ] Content trends in film and TV program genres, 1950s to 1980s
[ ] CATV; [ ] VHS; [ ] UHF; [ ] Prime Time Access Rule
[ ] film rating categories: G, PG, PG-13, R, NC-17; [ ] film sequels, rationale for
[ ] 1948 Paramount monopoly decision reversed: studios get back into the theater-owning business
[ ] VCRs, effects on the video and television industries
[ ] Low-power television (LPTV); [ ] direct broadcast satellite (DBS)
[ ] time shifting; [ ] zipping; [ ] zapping; [ ] grazing

TOPICS FOR DISCUSSION

1. Since movies are so expensive, it simply makes good business sense to build on proven winners such as films and stars that have already shown profitability at the box office. But while sequels may be wise choices for stockholders, what about people who want to experiment? How do we encourage creativity without gambling the farm? The same problem, of course, holds for TV.

2. What is your favorite old movie and movie star (be sensitive in your definition of "old" to students over 30 around you)?

3. Along the same line, (a) what was the best movie ever made? (b) what was the most socially influential movie ever made? Can you name any critically acclaimed foreign films?

4. What's the difference between a film reviewer and a film critic?

5. One recent survey suggested that *time shifting* would be even more prominent than it is, save for one thing: 60 percent of people who own VCRs have no idea how to program them. Do a quick poll to see if the same holds true in your own class (encourage frankness).

6. Films and TV have always reflected (some say led) changing social values and personal morals. Can you cite any films or TV shows that send opposing messages? In *ET* and *Close Encounters*, for example, the universe is "peopled" by good creatures; compare their message with *Alien*.

7. Cite examples of stereotypes still present in film or TV (by sex, race, ethnicity or other category).

8. Hollywood, theaters, and advertisers are gingerly experimenting with using soft-sell advertising before the feature show begins. Your feelings? More importantly, what could you do to show your displeasure, assuming you don't approve of the practice?

9. Jamie Lee Curtis and Sigourney Weaver are generally described as guaranteed box office draws. Kevin Costner, Tom Cruise, and Bruce Willis are also examples. But as Weaver points out in an interview, *male* stars usually command twice the salary of women. Why?

10. Do you agree with how movie critics rate films? Do you have a favorite critic that you usually agree with and therefore trust his or her judgement as to whether or not see a particular film?

11. To cut budgets, yet still attract audiences, TV networks and syndicates have turned to low-cost "trash TV," e.g., "tell all" talk shows, shock interviews, real life police stories, and date-a-person offerings. And the strategy, according to ratings, seems to be working. Is TV taking advantage of our base interests (much like sensationalistic newspapers of the 1890s)? Your views?

12. One of the highest rated (and oft imitated) TV shows is CBS's *60 Minutes*. What is the draw for TV investigative news shows? Do you think they're accurate? Sensationalistic?

13. Make a case pro or con: Is the quality of films and TV getting better--not just technically better, but qualitatively better (content caliber, acting, writing, creativity, and so on)?

Chapter 11: True/False Test

History of Film and Television

1. In reality, "motion" pictures aren't in motion at all. It's the illusion we get when we're exposed to still pictures flashing in front of our eyes at 30 frames per second; we call this phenomenon "persistence of vision."

2. Excesses in film content and star behavior in the 1920s led to government censorship of the film industry, with the FCC finally imposing the rating system of G, PG, R, and X in 1932.

3. They may have shown "silent" films, but silent-film theaters were rarely silent.

4. Hollywood's "studio years" were between 1930 and 1950.

5. The Prime Time Access Rule requires that local TV stations provide for their own programming between 7:30 and 8:00 P.M. EST.

6. The film industry, unlike other media, never fragmented its content to attract special audiences.

7. Reversing a trend that films "belonged" to teens, Hollywood now makes more mature-content movies as audiences begin to age and as teens continue to rent more films for VCR use at home.

8. TV's *adult western* genre didn't last long because of its heavy reliance on sex and raw language.

9. Many TV shows in the early 1950s were replanted directly from radio networks.

10. Regulation has gone full circle; since the 1980s, film companies may once again control their own production, distribution, and exhibition outlets.

11. LPTV is a broadcasting system designed to create neighborhood TV stations and markets.

12. The *star system* was the first attempt to rate films according to quality on a 1-to-5 star basis.

13. One of the chief problems with early TV was "storage," there being no way to save or edit a program for later broadcast.

14. UHF television channels are between 2 and 13.

15. Formula films and sequels essentially reflect a conservative economic philosophy.

Chapter 11: Multiple Choice Test

History of Film and Television

1. The _____ film genre was a unique contribution to movie making by the U.S. film industry.

    a. war
    b. slapstick

    c. western
    d. made-for-TV

2. Known simply as *Mr. Television*, he was probably responsible for selling more TV sets than anyone else.

    a. Ernie Kovacs
    b. Sid Caesar

    c. Johnny Carson
    d. Milton Berle

3. The content of early TV shows was heavily influenced, if not outright controlled, by the:

    a. networks
    b. affiliates

    c. advertisers
    d. Actors Guild

4. TV advertisers are least concerned about:

    a. zipping
    b. zapping

    c. the growth of cable TV
    d. grazing

5. Which of the below is *not* one of the film industry's three major components:

    a. production
    b. syndication

    c. distribution
    d. exhibition

6. It was the first full-length motion picture, now rarely shown because of its racist overtones.

    a. *The General*
    b. *Birth of a Nation*

    c. *In the Heat of the Night*
    d. *The Jazz Singer*

7. Which film doesn't belong to Hollywood's most "golden" period, 1939-1941?

    a. *Ben Hur*
    b. *The Wizard of Oz*

    c. *Gone with the Wind*
    d. *Citizen Kane*

8. Three of these items characterize today's film industry. Which doesn't?

   a. indulgent experimentation   c. ownership consolidation
   b. audience fragmentation   d. economic conservatism

9. Sequels are closest in purpose and nature to the _____ film.

   a. epic   c. double-feature
   b. formula   d. avant-garde

10. What solved TV's "storage" problem and saved it from always having to broadcast "live?"

   a. videotape   c. cable TV
   b. the kinetoscope   d. film

11. Hollywood used three of these ideas to lure audiences back to theaters and away from TV in the 1950s; which item doesn't belong?

   a. 3-D   c. Cinemascope
   b. sound   d. topics unsuitable for TV broadcast

12. Once the novelty of the first "physical action" films wore off, audiences in the 1910s weren't lured back in big numbers until the introduction of films that:

   a. used professional actors   c. told a story
   b. featured sound   d. lasted at least two hours

13. The most negative trend for TV networks recently is:

   a. advent of LPTV and HDTV   c. network mergers and takeovers
   b. remote-control grazing   d. audience "leakage" to cable TV and VCRs

14. In the 1950s, three of these were TV's mainline program genres; which doesn't belong?

   a. TV versions of radio programs c. sophisticated, high-quality dramas
   b. adult westerns   d. Oscar-level movie reruns

15. In the 1910s, many independent film makers moved to Hollywood. Which one of these items wasn't one of their reasons?

   a. to reduce labor costs   c. to find a place with good, dependable weather
   b. to get a variety of scenic backgrounds   d. to escape from the rules of the MPPC

16. The introduction of sound to film ultimately paid off, but there were many initial negative effects; not among them:

    a. many silent screen stars (due to poor voices) couldn't make the transition
    b. production costs skyrocketed
    c. location shooting became much more difficult
    d. movie attendance dropped sharply until sound tracks improved

17. Nickelodeons gave way to movie palaces for three main reasons; which answer doesn't belong?

    a. posh surroundings helped justify higher ticket prices needed to pay for higher production costs
    b. film actors demanded the same ornate atmosphere found in counterpart stage theaters
    c. people found it too uncomfortable to sit on wooden benches or seats for long films
    d. big theaters could seat hundreds more people at one sitting, thus more profits

18. Which of these was *not* a major program genre in 1950s TV?

    a. the adult western (*Gunsmoke*)   c. the variety show (*Ed Sullivan Show*)
    b. live dramatic plays (*Playhouse 90*)   d. investigative news programs (*60 Minutes*)

19. What program type proved to be a big embarrassment to the TV industry in the late 1950s?

    a. adult westerns   c. quiz shows
    b. radio transplants   d. musicals

20. Cable television (CATV) originally began:

    a. in order to bring TV programs into remote mountainous regions
    b. as a joint venture with AT&T and the local telephone companies
    c. in hopes of supplanting movie theaters
    d. as an experiment for two-way communication

CHAPTER 11: TEST ANSWER KEYS

True/False Test

01. True	05. True	09. True	13. True
02. False	06. False	10. True	14. False
03. True	07. True	11. True	15. True
04. True	08. False	12. False	

Multiple-Choice Test

01. C	06. B	11. B	16. D
02. D	07. A	12. C	17. B
03. C	08. A	13. D	18. D
04. C	09. B	14. D	19. C
05. B	10. A	15. A	20. A

-------------- **N O T E S** --------------

Chapter 12

Structure of the Motion Picture Industry

Some eighty years since it all began, the film industry has transformed itself several times over. Yet many things remain the same: a few corporations looking to dominate the field, highly talented artists looking to entertain, and a mass audience that still hasn't lost its appetite for fantasy and escapism. This chapter examines today's trends in the film industry's three main divisions: production, distribution, and exhibition. We'll see what's changed since the 1900s, why, how, and what may become of film's growing interdependence with TV.

CHAPTER OBJECTIVES

· know the major roles and job responsibilities in each of film's major divisions: production, distribution, and exhibition

· understand how a film goes from an idea on paper to the final product in theaters, cable, and cassette sales or rentals

KEY TERMS AND CONCEPTS

[ ] film industry structure: production, distribution and exhibition
[ ] production trends: more films, independents film makers dominate; new role of studios
[ ] distribution role: worldwide networks; print duplicating, advertising and promotion, financing
[ ] exhibition trends: more theaters; large chains; advent of the multiplex theater
[ ] ownership trends: foreign investors; conglomerate ownership
[ ] film stages: preproduction, production, and postproduction
[ ] property; [ ] option contract
[ ] filming sequence; [ ] average filming time and cost per day
[ ] dailies; [ ] average film length, reasons for
[ ] revenue sources (U.S. and foreign box office, VHS rental and sales, CATV and TV rights)
[ ] financing sources and methods:
    [ ] total loan   [ ] limited partnership
    [ ] pickup   [ ] joint venture
[ ] gross receipts split, who gets what first? [ ] the 2.5 x production cost = profit guideline
[ ] how exhibitors repay distributors: [ ] percentage splits; [ ] sliding scale; [ ] four-walling
[ ] theater concession stands profits
[ ] pricing strategies for cassette sales and rental (cf.. "sell through" markets)
[ ] growing role of PPV as an exhibition outlet; [ ] movies on demand

TOPICS FOR DISCUSSION

1. What book, story, or event do you think is a great movie idea just waiting to be discovered? Why? Who would you cast in the lead roles? Location? Target audience?

2. At what point in price do you say to a theater owner, "Your tickets are too expensive and your concessions are way overpriced; no thanks, I'll wait for the home video"?

3. Have cable, PPV, or cassette film sales/rentals significantly changed your movie habits? How? Do you see more movies today (one way or the other) than you did ten years ago?

4. What's the qualitative difference between viewing a film at the theater and at home? Does either have any kind of advantage over the other? Is "going to the show" really a social experience?

5. Your text mentions excessive violence as an important issue now confronting both the film and TV industries. Your opinions? Are there other excesses? Conversely, are there treatments or topics of which you don't see enough?

6. Discuss and defend you position on movie pirating (taping a film off cable, for example). Is it *really* stealing?

7. Reflect on the influence foreign ownership may have on American films. Do you believe some topics, approaches, or morals might be altered to suit the new home country's social values?

8. Though no one knows which films will succeed and which won't, Hollywood still tries its best to predict the outcome. In that vein, what chances did Kevin Costner take in terms of subject matter, film cost, and choice of star/director for *Waterworld?* Do you think his gamble paid off?

9. *Gone with the Wind* and *Citizen Kane* (each some fifty plus years old) are often named as the best films ever made; what would your top two choices be and why?

10. Have you ever seen a 3-D film? Aromarama? Cinerama? Sensorsound (*Earthquake* and *The Battle of Midway* were made for this one)? Cinemascope? Other special effects? Reactions?

11. The most notorious (and certainly longest running) cult film of all times is *The Rocky Horror Motion Picture Show* (usually shown only at midnight on Fridays). Devotees say its not the movie, but the theater experience that keeps this gem alive. Have you, or anyone you know, had the pleasure? Reactions?

12. Would you rather see an original movie most of the time or a good sequel to a successful film?

13. What changes would you incorporate into a new theater complex?

Chapter 12: True/False Test

Structure of the Motion Picture Industry

1. Independent producers, not studios, make the majority of films produced today.

2. While major conglomerates dominate film production and distribution systems, most theaters are still owned by small, independent owners.

3. Most films run about 100 minutes so that theaters have about 20 minutes to clear and fill seats between showings.

4. Films are shot sequentially, beginning to end, to preserve film continuity and to conserve expenses.

5. *Four-walling* a film is essentially like renting out a theater.

6. Studios generally decide the selling price of a film cassette this way: the more successful the film, the more expensive the video.

7. One major reason for PPV's lukewarm reception is that rental stores get their film copies about the same time (if not before) the film airs on PPV.

8. How well a movie does at the box office will be a direct reflection of how well--or poorly--it will do with cassette sales and rentals.

9. Most films continue to make more money at the box office than with cassette sales and rentals.

10. In the past, only 20 percent of most films made a profit; today that figure is closer to 60 percent.

11. Many theater owners make the majority of their profits through concession stand sales.

12. In general, a film needs to make about 2 ½ times its production costs before it turns a profit.

13. It takes an average of about six months to do the actual filming of a movie.

14. A book, before it might become a movie, is called an *option contract.*

15. The majority of film production companies in this country are still U.S. owned.

Chapter 12: Multiple Choice Test

Structure of the Motion Picture Industry

1. A major film distributor usually does all but which of the following?

    a. promotion
    b. finance

    c. distribution
    d. property screening

2. In the last ten years there have been increases in all but which of these areas?

    a. new theaters
    b. movies made

    c. box-office prices
    d. drive-ins

3. A book, a play, or any idea that might be an idea for a motion picture is called:

    a. an option contract
    b. a script

    c. a property
    d. a pickup

4. Big-name movie stars are paid:

    a. by set contractual fee
    b. in merchandising revenues

    c. as a percentage of film profits
    d. any of the above

5. The person in charge of actually making the film is the:

    a. film editor
    b. director

    c. cinematographer
    d. distributor

6. Beyond its obvious duties, this film department is also responsible for advertising and promoting a movie, duplicating the hundreds of necessary copies of a film and, on occasion, actually lending money to an independent producer to make a film.

    a. production
    b. distribution

    c. exhibition
    d. syndication

7. It takes about _____ days to film the average movie.

   a. 25
   b. 70

   c. 180
   d. 250

8. Who *normally* assumes the biggest financial risk in backing a film?

   a. the film's cast
   b. distributor

   c. director
   d. exhibitor

9. Identify this exhibition system: the bigger the box-office receipts, the greater the distributor's share of the take.

   a. sliding scale
   b. split percentage

   c. four-walling
   d. none of the above

10. When a distributor agrees to finance a producer's completed film for a set amount of money after a certain period of time, that arrangement is called a:

    a. pickup
    b. limited partnership

    c. joint venture
    d. none of the above

11. Which is *not* a major organizational part of the film industry?

    a. production
    b. distribution

    c. exhibition
    d. syndication

12. The biggest revenue source for most films today is from:

    a. U.S. box-office receipts
    b. cassette sales and rentals

    c. cable and TV rights
    d. foreign box-office receipts

13. A *sell-through* movie market is a:

    a. successful film that's being sold as a video and marketed to the public at affordable prices (usually $30 or less)
    b. theater where profits come mainly from the concession stand
    c. recent film released to the PPV market on a "show-only-once" basis
    d. film designed to make profits primarily through merchandise sales, e.g., *Pocahontas, The Lion King, Casper,* and the *Batman* films.

14. *Dailies* are the _____ which the director reviews at the end of day.

    a. film's shooting schedule
    b. day's completed film footage
    c. expense reports for a film shooting day
    d. dialogue and script changes

15. Common Hollywood wisdom holds that a film must make _____ times its production costs before it starts to show a profit.

    a. 1 to 1½
    b. 2 to 2 ½
    c. 4 to 6
    d. at least 10

16. Dialogue retakes, special effect add ins, film editing, sound effects, and narrative voice overs take place in a film's _____ stage.

    a. production
    b. postproduction
    c. exhibition
    d. treatment

17. Which of the following is not true concerning the state of today's film industry?

    a. independent companies now produce about 2/3 of all U.S. films made
    b. film production is up, over 25 percent since 1982
    c. opulent movie theaters that can hold over 2,000 people are making a comeback
    d. a record number of movie theater screens has created a demand for movies that the major distributors can't handle, the slack now being handled by independent distributors

18. Execution of an *option contract* would happen in which stage of a film's history?

    a. preproduction
    b. production
    c. postproduction
    d. exhibition

19. An average, moderate-budget film costs about _____ per day to shoot.

    a. $50,000
    b. $150,000
    c. $325,000
    d. $1,000,000

20. If you wanted to get together with a few other individuals to help finance a movie, you would probably enter into an arrangement that's known as a(n) _____ .

    a. option contract
    b. limited partnership
    c. joint venture
    d. percentage split

CHAPTER 12:   TEST ANSWER KEYS

True/False Test

01. True	05. True	09. False	13. False
02. False	06. False	10. True	14. False
03. True	07. True	11. True	15. False
04. False	08. False	12. True	

Multiple-Choice Test

01. D	06. B	11. D	16. B
02. D	07. B	12. B	17. C
03. C	08. B	13. A	18. A
04. D	09. A	14. B	19. C
05. B	10. A	15. B	20. B

-------------- **N O T E S** --------------

Chapter 13

Structure of the Television Industry

Like a quiet country store that turned into the Wal-Mart chain, TV just isn't the simple little thing it once was. This chapter highlights the enormous changes still taking place in an industry that's been fragmented, merged, regulated, reinvented, praised, and cursed--all several times over.

CHAPTER OBJECTIVES

. learn the major systems by which TV is delivered, operated, owned, and funded

. note how audiences are changing TV by how and when they use it

KEY TERMS AND CONCEPTS

[ ] commercial TV system: FCC licensed, 211 U.S. markets, network affiliates v independents
[ ] six commercial networks: CBS, ABC, NBC (about 200 affiliates each), FBC, UPN, and WBN
[ ] PBS: noncommercial network; [ ] industry organization: production, distribution, exhibition
[ ] program sources: local (news is biggest expense and revenue source), syndication, and networks
[ ] distribution sources: networks, cable networks, and syndication companies
[ ] network-affiliate contracts: who pays whom for what, and why?
[ ] syndicate contract types: [ ] straight cash; [ ] cash plus barter; [ ] barter arrangement
[ ] deficit-cost programming: the aftermarket syndication gamble; [ ] the 100th episode milepost
[ ] VHF (2-13) and UHF (14-69): differences between and profiles of (especially independents)
[ ] FCC's 1984 ownership regulation change: the "12-station, 25 percent" rule, consequences of
[ ] *station* organization: sales, engineering , production, news, administration
[ ] *networks*: sales, entertainment, O&Os, affiliate relations, news, sports, standards, operations
[ ] prime time (8-11 P.M., EST; [ ] pilot
[ ] programming strategies: audience flow; counter-programming; challenge programming
[ ] advertising types: [ ] national; [ ] national spot; [ ] local
[ ] how TV ad rates are determined: market size and program ratings
[ ] CPB and PBS: current trends, funding problems and sources
[ ] Cable TV: history (major trends: regulation, audience fragmentation, ownership consolidation
[ ] CATV organization: head end, distribution system, and house drop; [ ] programming sources
[ ] local cable income sources: subscription fees and local advertising; [ ] carriage fee
[ ] national cable revenue sources: advertising, carriage fees, and subscription fees
[ ] timeshifting; [ ] VCR use, profile of; [ ] TV satellite delivery: 6-foot and 18-inch systems
[ ] HDTV; [ ] scan lines; [ ] screen aspect ratio (current: 3x4; HDTV: 9x16)
[ ] cable compression, effects of; [ ] holography

TOPICS FOR DISCUSSION

1. List everything you use your TV set for, from network broadcasts to home video games to closed-circuit monitors. Do a class poll on the range and frequency of how TV's are used.

2. Historians might record the TV remote control as one of our most insidious inventions. It gives us more convenience, but only at the price of increased temptation. On the whole, are remote control devices time wasters or time savers? And are remote control devices a "male thing?"

3. Should the government continue to license broadcast stations? How does licensing reconcile with our free speech values? Why aren't cable networks subject to licensing?

4. Cable, VCRs, DBS, PPV, cassette rentals--these new developments all share a common theme: they're only good for people who can afford them. But what about the millions of Americans who can't afford them? It's not just the entertainment they're missing, but education, news, political debates, and so on. Can we tolerate a society of information "haves" and "have nots?"

5. Would you buy an 18-inch satellite dish system? If so, would you keep your cable system too?

6. Your list of favorite books, magazines, music, and films says a lot about your personal tastes. But what about favorite TV shows? What are your Top Ten favorites? There's an old adage that says "You are what you eat." What about TV; are you "what you watch?"

7. Contest: name as many subject-specific cable TV channels as you can.

8. An average home has a TV on about seven plus hours a day. The figure increases yearly, yet few people admit to watching that much TV. How much daily TV do you think is excessive?

9. Do people use TV as a baby sitter--to excess--for kids? Was it ever used that way with you?

10. Why do soap operas continue to be so popular (first in radio, now as the leading use for VCR timeshifting)? Which mass media functions do they provide? Fess up; what's your favorite one?

11. CompuServe, a national computer database, advertises itself as an "information utility;" much like gas, water and electricity. Would you now consider cable TV a utility?

12. A recent poll revealed an interesting statistic: the more money you earn, the less TV you watch. Explain the possible reasons.

13. This is a harder task than you think: name the top three things you like about TV; now name the top three things you don't.

Chapter 13: True/False Test

Structure of the Television Industry

1. A TV affiliate gets about 30 percent of its programming from its parent network.

2. ABC, CBS, and NBC each have about 200 affiliate stations.

3. TV networks pay affiliates for airing network shows during prime time; the bigger the market, the more money the affiliate gets.

4. A TV syndicate gives an independent TV station the exclusive right, but for a limited number of times, to air a leased program within that independent's market area.

5. Most prime-time network series don't break even with what they cost to make; the production companies gamble that they can make up the difference later in the syndication aftermarket.

6. The FCC has no regulatory authority over cable television.

7. *Program flow* is a technique used to keep viewers tuned to the same station, e.g., a sitcom flows into another sitcom or an action series feeds into another action series.

8. "Free" cable channels, such as CNN, MTV, or A&E only look free because you never see the individual carriage fees on your bill that your local cable outlet pays to get those channels.

9. Unlike local stations, cable companies are restricted from offering local origination programming.

10. Prime time is 7-10 P.M., EST.

11. HDTV screens look rectangular (like a film screen) as opposed to the boxy look of current TV.

12. The cable wire that comes into your home from a feeder line is called a *head end*.

13. For most commercial TV stations, news is both their biggest programming expense and their biggest revenue source.

14. TV advertising rates are determined by two things: market size and program ratings.

15. An affiliate station is more likely to use a syndicate's services than an independent station..

Chapter 13:   Multiple-Choice Test

Structure of the Television Industry

1. The most profitable types of local-originated TV programs are:

   a. talk shows
   b. public affair specials

   c. news
   d. sports

2. Independent TV production firms sell their programs to:

   a. broadcast networks
   b. syndicates

   c. cable networks
   d. all the above

3. What essentially "saved" UHF stations, giving them almost equal exposure as the VHF stations?

   a. federal subsidies
   b. popular network reruns

   c. alternative programming
   d. when they began being carried by cable TV

4. Which of these isn't a reason for broadcast network "audience slide"?

   a. growth of cable industry
   b. timeshifting

   c. increased VCR use for viewing movies
   d. stronger UHF competition

5. PBS stations get the *least* of their revenues from:

   a. government subsidies
   b. local advertisers

   c. corporate grants
   d. subscriber donations

6. FCC regulations now limit anyone from owning more than _____ TV stations, provided further that collectively they do not reach more than _____ percent of all U.S. households.

   a. 10 and 10
   b. 12 and 25

   c. 20 and 40
   d. 50 and 50

7. The first episode of a potential TV series is called a:

a. leader
b. shooter

c. head end
d. pilot

8. The revenue for a premium cable network can come from _____ charges.

a. carriage fees
b. subscription fees

c. advertising
d. all the above

9. *Head end, distribution system*, and *house drop* are the three main components of:

a. TV syndicates
b. network feed systems

c. cable TV systems
d. a satellite dish network

10. HDTV gets its superior picture quality because it:

a. nearly doubles the number of screen scan lines for a sharper picture resolution
b. increases the current base of 64-colors to 256 colors
c. uses fiber optic cable to deliver its signal (as opposed to over-the-air transmission)
d. employs holographic techniques to supply a 3-D quality to images

11. Which of the below is *not* a TV programming strategy:

a. audience flow
b. audience fragmentation

c. counter-programming
d. challenge programming

12. Assume you are the program director of a local independent TV station. A syndicate firm offers you a program series for the following terms: a limited amount of cash plus a certain amount of air time in which they can air their own commercials. This type of an arrangement is called a:

a. straight cash deal
b. cash plus barter contract

c. barter agreement
d. carriage fee

13. There appears to be a minimum number of programs a syndicate needs in order to successfully market reruns of a popular TV series. That number is:

a. 25
b. 50

c. 100
d. 250

14. The audience size of a TV station's viewing area varies, of course, depending upon where that station is located. The FCC breaks the U.S. into 211 of these "areas," which we call:

   a. markets   c. affiliates
   b. domains   d. tracts

15. Which of the below is the biggest noncommercial network in the U.S.?

   a. FBC   c. PBS
   b. UPN   d. WBN

16. Affiliate Relations, O&Os, and Standards. You'll only find these departments in a _____ organization.

   a. cable   c. syndicate
   b. broadcast network   d. public broadcasting

17. As an advertiser, if you only wanted your message to go to Western mountain states, you'd most likely buy what form of advertisement?

   a. national   c. local
   b. syndicated   d. national spot

18. The bottom fell out of this device when many networks began to scramble their signals:

   a. HDTV   c. TVROs (6-foot satellite dish receivers)
   b. 18-inch satellite dish receivers d. Community Antenna TV

19. Which of these program types is timeshifted most?

   a. soap operas   c. network news
   b. game shows   d. sitcoms

20. Which of these doesn't currently appear to be a major trend in the TV industry?

   a. greater audience fragmentation   c. corporate consolidations
   b. increasing federal regulation   d. expanding program delivery systems

CHAPTER 13:   TEST ANSWER KEYS

True/False Test

01.	False	05.	True	09.	False	13.	True
02.	True	06.	False	10.	False	14.	True
03.	True	07.	True	11.	True	15.	False
04.	True	08.	True	12.	False		

Multiple-Choice Test

01.	C	06.	B	11.	B	16.	B
02.	D	07.	D	12.	B	17.	D
03.	D	08.	D	13.	C	18.	C
04.	B	09.	C	14.	A	19.	A
05.	B	10.	A	15.	C	20.	B

-------------- **N O T E S** --------------

Chapter 14

Computers and Mass Communications

This chapter scratches the surface of a mass medium (computer communications) that's literally being built as you read this sentence. Taking a ride down the information highway (technologically, still more like a dirt road than an eight-lane expressway), we'll examine the landscape of potential improvements to individual and global communications. You'll notice that the list of questions and concerns about this form of communication seems longer than the promises it seems to hold for us; and perhaps that's as it should be, for with no other form of communication have individuals had the power to help build a medium as we have with the Internet. We'll end with a look at undoubtedly one of the most intriguing and potentially useful (some say harmful) emerging technologies--virtual reality-- and what it might mean for your personal and professional future.

CHAPTER OBJECTIVES

- ponder the many directions individuals, society, culture, and politics might take as we build the information highway

- understand the history, purpose, features, and functions of the Internet and online PC services

- explore the pros and cons of the powerful world of virtual reality

KEY TERMS AND CONCEPTS

[ ] information highway
[ ] telecommuting
[ ] computer history, major trends
[ ] modems
[ ] Internet, definition; [ ] Net statistics: number of networks, PC host systems, number of users,
[ ] Internet, historical reasons for formation
[ ] Internet feature areas: [ ] e-mail; [ ] Telenet; [ ] Newsgroups; [ ] World Wide Web
[ ] newsgroup "threads"; [ ] binary code
[ ] hypertext; [ ] Local Area Networks (LANs)
[ ] netiquette
[ ] placing advertising on the Internet, views of users about
[ ] on-line information companies: Prodigy, CompuServe, America Online, GEnie, and Delphi
[ ] virtual reality; [ ] technorot
[ ] social implications of the computer as a mass media vehicle

TOPICS FOR DISCUSSION

1. Pretend you could slip into a virtual reality world of your own making that was--at least in terms of excitement, adventure, or romance--more engaging than your "real" world. Now assume you could also have "virtual friends" that could share the fun of that world with you. Do you see any danger of emotionally or intellectually dropping out of our world in favor of a cyberspace one?

2. Would you be a good candidate for telecommuting? What might that practice do to a marriage? Or to rush hour? Would you consider telecommuting to college? Pros and cons?

3. In 1995 *Time* magazine published an extensive examination of sex in cyberspace. Although you won't see the online services boast about it, cybersex is a big hit with computer users. *Hot chat*, as it's called, is one of the most popular uses for real-time online conversations between people. Is this a harmless practice? What about the dangers of deception or access by children?

4. Express your views about electronic information access as a "right" for U.S. citizens, regardless of their ability to pay for it. Can we afford--culturally or ethically--a nation of information *haves* and *have nots*?

5. Should Internet and online research skills be taught in schools? If so, when? If not, why not?

6. Do a class poll; how many students have access to an online service at home or at school? Does anyone in class have an Internet e-mail address? How many of you have ever "surfed the net?"

7. Can you cite any examples of *technorot* (defined as the time when technology actually interferes with personal or business productivity instead of enhancing it)? Then--in all frankness--answer if it was really the technology at fault or a person who simply didn't understand the technology.

8. Do you know of any technophobic people? In an age of information access, might they truly be called "handicapped" and deserving of special help, psychological or instructional?

9. Statistics say computers are in about 20 percent of American households. What is that figure for your class? Assuming it's a higher percentage (it should be), do you see any correlation between computer ownership and upward mobility (being able to go to college)?

10. Calculators wiped out slide rulers almost overnight (if you don't know what a slide ruler is/was, ask your instructor). Likewise, computers and word processing software have made typewriters just as obsolete and almost as quickly. Might e-mail make the U.S. Post Office obsolete in the same manner? (Give the packages to UPS and Federal Express) Might there be any other older technologies on the brink of extinction because of computers?

11. Should information (or, for that matter, electronically delivered entertainment) be considered a household "utility" in the same sense as gas, water, and electricity? Isn't access to information just as critical for our cultural survival as a warm house in winter is to our physical survival?

Chapter 14: True/False Test

Computers and Mass Communications

1. The Internet is owned by a multinational conglomerate.

2. Currently the information highway network exists only in the United States, but experts predict it will go global by 2005.

3. *Telecommuting* is a system of two-way interactive television (also known as teleconferencing).

4. The Internet is essentially impossible to censor.

5. *Modems* are devices that link one computer to another via telephone lines.

6. The first computers were mechanical devices, not electronic ones.

7. The binary code, the numerical system upon which all digital communications rests, is made up of only two electronic signals: "on" or "off," which are then interpreted as standing for a 0 or 1.

8. ARPANET, the forerunner to the Internet, was a network of interconnected computers designed so that the system--as a whole--could withstand a nuclear attack.

9. The informal agreement of *do's* and *don'ts* for network communicating is called *netiquette*.

10. Collectively, the online services (Prodigy, CompuServe, etc.) make up the Internet.

11. The term *virtual reality* is an oxymoron, i.e., the terms are mutually contradictory.

12. The Internet is headquartered in New York City.

13. It's envisioned that the information highway will deliver information, education, entertainment, commercial services, teleconferencing, mail, and phone service (to name only a few things); the Internet, however, will be limited to providing only information and educational resources.

14. To experience virtual reality you don't need to wear special equipment, but you do need to be in a special room closed off from outside light or noises.

15. Most Internet users don't mind online ads, as long as they're unobtrusive and soft-sell in nature.

Chapter 14:   Multiple-Choice Test

Computers and Mass Communications

1. Which Internet feature below allows your computer to use the facilities of another computer?

   a. e-mail
   b. Telnet

   c. Newsgroups
   d. World Wide Web (WWW)

2. Which of these devices serves as a telephone interface, allowing your PC to "talk" with another?

   a. scanner
   b. modem

   c. fiber optic cable
   d. local area network

3. If you wanted to "hang out" with other people that had similar interests, which Internet area would you most likely visit?

   a. e-mail
   b. World Wide Web

   c. Telnet
   d. Newsgroups

4. Hypertext, a way of quickly accessing related information, is found on what part of the Internet?

   a. e-mail
   b. World Wide Web

   c. Telnet
   d. Newsgroups

5. A group of nearby computers electronically linked together (as in an office or school setting) is called a(n):

   a. binary system
   b. online database

   c. local area network (LAN)
   d. ARPANET

6. A note sent by e-mail from the United States to Japan would probably take about _____ to reach its destination.

   a. a few seconds
   b. 45 minutes

   c. a few hours
   d. 10-15 hours

7. Which of the below is currently *not* a criticism of the Internet?

   a. it's still a difficult system for most people to navigate, i.e., to find what you're looking for
   b. the information and pictures it contains can be sexist, racist, violent, and pornographic
   c. it cannot be politically censored
   d. without gatekeepers, it's susceptible to misinformation and a glut of data trivia

8. In the 1991 Persian Gulf War, Iraq used _____ to keep its command and control computer system in operation despite heavy U.S. bombing.

   a. the Internet
   b. virtual reality

   c. a local area network
   d. the World Wide Web

9. It was the _____ that created its own computer network to link five supercomputers together that actually began what we know today as the Internet.

   a. Department of Defense
   b. Department of Education

   c. World Wide Web
   d. National Science Foundation

10. Three of these items are characteristics of a virtual reality environment; which one isn't?

   a. creates computer-generated images of a 360-degree, 3-D environment
   b. usually requires the user to wear a special helmet
   c. user often able to manipulate objects within a VR environment using special gloves
   d. many people can interact within a VR environment simultaneously

11. Which of the below is currently not a social concern about the Internet?

   a. it's outpaced legislation, giving rise to concerns about copyright, libel, and pornography issues
   b. it may encourage escapism, taking people away from the *real* world and productive activities
   c. anyone can "log on," regardless of nationality
   d. it may qualitatively diminish the surveillance and interpretive functions of existing mass media

12. "Universal access" is a concept intended to:

   a. insure that anyone--rich or poor, PC literate or not--has access to the information highway
   b. give everyone on the planet access to a computer within a one-mile walking range
   c. supply public information to anyone who wants it, regardless of their country of origin
   d. provide free access to any online database, commercial and noncommercial alike

13. Which of the below is *not* a commercial online database?

    a. Interramp   c. Prodigy
    b. America Online   d. CompuServe

14. Which of these descriptions doesn't belong? The Internet is:

    a. global   c. decentralized
    b. based in the U.S.   d. a network of networks

15. Experts estimate that about _____ people now use the Internet.

    a. 750,000   c. 30 million
    b. five million   d. 1.5 billion

16. A number of Newsgroup messages about the same subtopic is called:

    a. a thread   c. a web
    b. hypertext   d. a chat relay

17. If you want to officially complain about something on the Internet, you can call:

    a. the FCC   c. the Internet Society
    b. the telephone company   d. no one; no one has any regulatory authority

18. *Technorot* occurs when:

    a. computer systems "crash"   c. technology gets in the way of efficiency
    b. online data gets unusably old d. people get abusive online

19. As of 1994, and increasing daily, the Internet connected more than _____ computer networks.

    a. 750   c. 5000
    b. 1000   d. 18,000

20. Though growing quickly, commercial databases like Prodigy, CompuServe, and America Online are still owned by small companies, each network boasting about 250,000 members.

    a. True   b. False

CHAPTER 14:   TEST ANSWER KEYS

True/False Test

01. False	05. True	09. True	13. False
02. False	06. True	10. False	14. False
03. False	07. True	11. True	15. False
04. True	08. True	12. False	

Multiple-Choice Test

01. B	06. A	11. C	16. A
02. B	07. C	12. A	17. D
03. D	08. A	13. A	18. C
04. B	09. D	14. B	19. D
05 . C	10. D	15. C	20. B

-------------- **N O T E S** --------------

Chapter 15

News Gathering and Reporting

This chapter gives you a fascinating behind-the-scenes look at why the news that you read or see is especially selected, written, and packaged specifically for the medium in which you'll read or see it. We'll examine how emerging electronic and satellite capabilities are transforming the definition of what constitutes TV news, and how that transformation could even affect the need for network news.

CHAPTER OBJECTIVES

. learn the criteria (news values) that answer the question, "What is news?"

. see why print and broadcast news may give you the same news, but often in very different ways

. study the roles of key print and TV news personnel and the traditional wire services

KEY TERMS AND CONCEPTS

[ ] news values: timeliness, proximity, prominence, consequence, and human interest
[ ] news formats: print's "inverted pyramid"; [ ] the lead; [ ] broadcast's "square" format
[ ] TV news "sweep weeks," how news emphasis changes during
[ ] news categories: [ ] hard news; [ ] soft news (features); [ ] investigative reporting
[ ] *newsroom staff:* editors: managing, city, wire, copy; general assignment and beat reporters
[ ] *broadcast newsroom staff:* news director, executive and program producers, assignment editor, on-air reporters, anchors, tape editors, and writers, duties of
[ ] wire services: United Press International (UP) and Associated Press (AP)
[ ] group-newspaper wire services; [ ] major foreign wire services: Reuters, Agence-France
[ ] print v broadcast news, strengths and weaknesses of
[ ] news consultants: what they do; changes they bring about
[ ] electronic news gathering (ENG); [ ] satellite news gathering (SNG)
[ ] going live (physical, ethical, and accuracy), dangers of
[ ] SNG's new influence on local news programs; Conus and Newssource
[ ] journalistic principles: honesty, accuracy, balance, objectivity
[ ] issues: TV news v entertainment shows

TOPICS FOR DISCUSSION

1. Is there danger in giving the public what it wants in terms of news coverage? Isn't it the job of journalists to decide what people *need to* know instead of giving audiences what they *want*?

2. We often blast the media for reporting too much negative news. But is it the messengers' fault, or is that there *is* so much negative news? Would you rather there be a "good news" station?

3. Attribution answers the question, "Says who?" You've been doing that in term papers with source citations. So what is your opinion on the use of anonymous news sources, e.g., "a government official said . . ." or "a local critic said . . ."? And what if that's the only way the reporter can get a story?

4. Which is the most credible news medium: print or TV? Why?

5. Oliver Stone's film *JFK* received widespread kudos and criticism for the particular facts he used and how he presented them (gatekeeping). Do you think film should be in the news business?

6. The "public's right to know" is not directly stated in the U.S. Constitution; however, do you think we have that right? If not, why or when not? Who has the right to deny us that right?

7. Why is it impossible to be truly objective? Should a news report be balanced? Should the "bad guys or bad side" get equal coverage?

8. Why don't we see many older TV anchors? Unattractive ones? Heavy ones? How important are good looks to TV news ratings?

9. One reason that long investigative pieces are often discouraged is that supposedly the audiences get bored quickly--regardless of the significance or consequence of the story. Do you agree? Does news today need to be both entertaining *and* short?

10. Can you remember any story that a newspaper and a TV station reported in significantly different ways? What news medium--print or broadcast--do you think is better, and why?

11. Assume you're the editor of your college newspaper. You have ten reporters. Like a general with his troops, how would you deploy them to cover your entire college community? Which "beats" would you create? How many reporters for general assignment? Investigative reports?

12. Where would you rank journalism as a profession today in terms of prestige? The Top 10? 50? Give your reasons why. Where, by the way, would you rank your future profession?

Chapter 15: True/False Test

News Gathering and Reporting

1. Investigative reporting is increasingly discouraged because it tends to be expensive, time consuming, and not always fruitful.

2. The who, what, when, why, where, and how of a story is usually found in the first paragraph.

3 . All things being equal, the closer you live to an event the more important it becomes to you.

4. In general, print media no longer "break" stories; instead, they provide follow-up, depth, and expanded coverage.

5. While live news coverage may add a measure of immediacy, it inhibits the gatekeeping function; the dramatic visual often substitutes for perspective, balance, and significance.

6. The news gathering process is one of the few areas of mass media that has yet to be adversely affected by economic considerations.

7. Successful news programs like *60 Minutes*, *20/20*, and *Prime Time* cost much more to produce than prime time dramatic shows like *E.R.* or *NYPD Blue.*

8. Hard news stories are reported like traditional narrative, with a beginning, a middle, and an end.

9. You'll find the *lead* of a news story at the bottom of the inverted pyramid writing format.

10. Soft news leads are usually designed to tease and entice rather than present straight facts.

11. Investigative reporting is the modern equivalent of muckraking.

12. A "beat reporter" is tongue-in-cheek slang for the person who covers the music industry.

13. The Associated Press (AP) serves only the print media; United Press International, on the other hand, serves both print *and* broadcast media.

14. Print journalists tend to remain nameless, while TV reporters become well-known personalities.

15. Satellite news gathering capabilities may diminish the reliance of local stations on network news teams for covering geographically distant stories .

Chapter 15: Multiple-Choice Test

News Gathering and Reporting

1. A story about a telephone rate hike for both commercial and residential customers has which *primary* news value?

   a. consequence
   b. proximity

   c. timeliness
   d. prominence

2. The facts that reporters report, and the stories editors decide to print, are examples of the _____ _____ process.

   a. gatekeeping
   b. news gathering

   c. agenda setting
   d. news balancing

3. A news story about a "topless" car washing service would most likely air on TV during:

   a. the 12 A.M. - 6 A.M. slot
   b. late evening

   c. a "sweeps week"
   d. late afternoon slot

4. Who is normally in charge of selecting and assigning local news stories in a television newsroom?

   a. city editor
   b. news director

   c. assignment editor
   d. managing editor

5. Which of the items below is *not* a reason for writing stories in the inverted pyramid format?

   a. conveys most important information first
   b. story can be cut from bottom without losing vital facts
   c. facilitates greater accuracy and objectivity
   d. emphasizes the primary news value

6. The news value that all hard news stories share in common is:

   a. timeliness
   b. proximity

   c. consequence
   d. human interest

7. Determine--for your current situation--the *primary* news value of this story:

GRAYSLAKE, Ill. (AP) Some 75 college students burned their mass communication textbooks today in protest over excessive tests given by their instructor.

a. psychological proximity
b. consequence
c. prominence
d. timeliness

8. Which of these is the *oldest* item in the TV news tool kit?

a. film reports
b. satellite news gathering (SNG)
c. electronic news gathering (ENG)
d. videotape

9. Three of the below items are distinct advantages that newspapers have over broadcast news; find the one that's not.

a. in-depth coverage
b. greater news volume
c. permanency
d. immediacy

10. TV news has several advantages over newspapers; which of these isn't an advantage?

a. in-depth analysis
b. personalized reporting
c. visual drama
d. immediacy

11. News that focuses on money, sex, oddity, animals, children, trivia, health, etc., usually have what primary news value?

a. consequence
b. human interest
c. timeliness
d. prominence

12. A reporter assigned to cover a specific topic or area (police, fire, city hall, education, etc.) is called a _____ reporter.

a. general assignment
b. investigative
c. beat
d. interpretive

13. Journalists strive for several basic qualities in news stories; which is *not* considered one of them?

a. balance
b. drama
c. accuracy
d. objectivity

14. Who is responsible for writing the following story:

    WASHINGTON, D.C. (AP)--American students aren't watching quite as much television as they once did, but they're also spending less time reading, either for school or pleasure. . . .

    a. a state reporter
    b. a government official

    c. a wire service reporter
    d. a *Washington Post* writer

15. Gatekeeping occurs not only in content *selection,* but also in content *delivery;* news anchors could use their unique position to influence news delivery by using which of these devices?

    a. tone
    b. emphasized words or pauses

    c. facial expressions
    d. all the above

16. The most vital asset a news organization has is its:

    a. informants
    b. reporting talent

    c. credibility
    d. profitability

17. Filmed news reports were made obsolete by:

    a. satellite news gathering (SNG)
    b. Polaroid cameras

    c. wire-service photographs
    d. electronic news gathering (ENG)

18. Which of the below would you *least* likely see on the front page of a newspaper?

    a. wire-service reports
    b. feature stories, or soft news

    c. hard news
    d. investigative reports

19. Three of these devices makes it easy to skim your newspaper to determine what you want to read; one device doesn't. Which?

    a. tease leads
    b. hard-news lead

    c. inverted-pyramid format
    d. headlines

20. Television news stations are finding it easier to send reporters overseas to cover the local angle for news stories that affect their particular audiences. What's making this possible?

    a. increased profits
    b. super-fast films

    c. satellite news gathering systems
    d. video cameras

CHAPTER 15: TEST ANSWER KEYS

True/False Test

01. True	05. True	09. False	13. False
02. True	06. False	10. True	14. True
03. True	07. False	11. True	15. True
04. True	08. False	12. False	

Multiple-Choice Test

01. A	06. A	11. B	16. C
02. A	07. A	12. C	17. D
03. C	08. A	13. B	18. B
04. C	09. D	14. C	19. A
05. C	10. A	15. D	20. C

-------------- **N O T E S** --------------

Chapter 16

Structure of the Public Relations Industry

This chapter takes a brief look at the birth and development of mass media's newest auxiliary partner: public relations. We'll examine how PR personnel counsel top management, serving as liaisons between the parent organization, the public, and the press. Then we'll take a look at the typical four-part PR campaign strategy that helps organizations set and reach goals through a planning concept known as management by objectives (MBO).

CHAPTER OBJECTIVES

. learn the key distinctions among public relations, publicity, and advertising

. understand the classic four-part approach to a PR campaign

. appreciate the reasons behind the continuing growth of, and need for, a public relations industry since World War II

KEY TERMS AND CONCEPTS

[ ] PR definition, see p. 380 (distinctions between *press agency, publicity,* and *advertising*)
[ ] functions: public relations is a management function, advertising is a marketing function
[ ] profile: what people in PR usually do: public opinion, communications, management councilors
[ ] PR publics: internal, external, and inherent subgroups; [ ] PR as two-way communication
[ ] Ivy Lee; [ ] Edward L. Bernays
[ ] major reasons for PR's growth since WWII:
    [ ] recognition of corporate need to be socially responsible to the public
    [ ] consumer movement
    [ ] need for dedicated PR department to overcome complexities of big business or government
    [ ] corporate need to track quickly changing needs and opinions of increasingly complex publics
[ ] spin doctor
[ ] internal v external PR departments: [ ] organization; [ ] advantages and disadvantages of each
[ ] major areas where public relations is utilized
[ ] four-steps to effective PR: information gathering, planning, communication, and evaluation
[ ] planning types: [ ] strategic; [ ] tactical; [ ] management by objectives (MBO)
[ ] video news releases (VNRs)
[ ] general economic trends for PR; [ ] integrated marketing communications (IMC), issues with

TOPICS FOR DISCUSSION

1. If a PR's first loyalty is to management, how credible are its public messages?

2. As budget-starved news organizations continue to increase their reliance on information supplied by PR departments (especially with VNRs), do journalists risk losing their own credibility?

3. Reporters depend on the company they work for to earn a living, yet they profess independence from company influence where news judgment is concerned. A PR person (answering only to management) might make the same claim of professional independence. Is there a difference?

4. Why do you think PR is usually taught under the umbrella of journalism rather than business?

5. In a sense, don't we all practice personal public relations? Think of the ways you might improve your "image" through an effective PR campaign. Have you ever put a "spin" on a negative personal situation to improve *its* image?

6. Street wisdom holds an abundance of advice that sounds remarkably like PR mandates, e.g.:

    - Always put your best foot forward.
    - Look for the silver lining around a dark cloud.
    - Try to make the best of a bad situation.

    Can you think of others? Is there danger in any of this advice?

7. All things considered, is there *really* a fundamental difference between public relations and advertising? Is there a similar difference between public relations and propaganda? And is propaganda a *good* thing or a *bad* thing? Defend your position beyond personal feelings.

8. Assume you're a high-level, well-paid PR worker; and, realistically, if you lost this job you may not be able to find another. At what point then would you draw the line at not doing/saying something you thought was unethical? Give examples of where your personal principles would supersede job demands.

9. Some experts estimate that 40 percent of a newspaper's editorial material is rooted, directly or indirectly, in PR-supplied information. Do you think you've ever seen examples of that?

10. A common mistake is to equate PR with publicity; however, many individuals and corporations hire PR firms with the exact opposite goal, i.e., to keep them *out* of the news. For example, when is the last time you heard anything about an arms factory? Can you think of other firms, groups, and people who would probably prefer a low public profile?

11. Defend your position. Which is better, the typical PR company position or the IMC approach?

111

Chapter 16: True/False Test

Structure of the Public Relations Industry

1. *Publicity* is synonymous with *public relations*.

2. Historically, a company's PR director reports to the director of marketing.

3. PR is a two-way communication process; publicity, by contrast, is usually a one-way process.

4. A spin doctor's job is to put the best light on an issue (from his/her client's point of view).

5. Public relations, like advertising, targets only publics that are external to the organization.

6. Strategic planning is to *what* as tactical planning is to *how*.

7. PR campaigns routinely use advertising techniques to further their goals.

8. MBO stands for "marketing by organization."

9. A press agent's usual job is to generate publicity.

10. The number of PR *publics,* internal or external, is determined by the number of different groups affected by an organization's operations, decisions, or policies.

11. PR people are primarily "fire fighters" who help minimize the damage to an organization caused by adverse events.

12. The U.S. government, by law, is forbidden to influence public opinion by using PR organizations or techniques.

13. If the integrated marketing communications (IMC) people had their way, the PR department's staff would report to the director of marketing (with advertising, PR, and marketing functions being more or less united under one departmental roof).

14. Video news releases (VNRs) are rarely used by TV news staffs; instead, VNRs are mainly made for internal company use and showings by public organizations (schools, libraries, and so on).

15. PR people are mass media generalists, i.e., they need to understand each medium in order to best know how and when to use each medium.

Chapter 16: Multiple-Choice Test

Structure of the Public Relations Industry

1. Which of these does *not* accurately describe public relations? Public relations:

   a. is usually a management function
   b. sometimes uses interpersonal communication
   c. attempts to persuade, often using mass media vehicles
   d. is used by advertising departments to ultimately further marketing ends (sales)

2. A public relations campaign would *most* likely try to influence:

   a. government legislators
   b. corporate management
   c. an organization's publics
   d. mass media outlets

3. The MBO process belongs predominately to the _____ stage of PR campaigns.

   a. information gathering
   b. planning
   c. communication
   d. evaluation

4. Which of these wouldn't be (or at least shouldn't be) a PR target public?

   a. employees
   b. stockholders
   c. the organization's publics
   d. management

5. Evaluation of a PR campaign is impossible without:

   a. information gathering
   b. campaign objectives
   c. feedback
   d. all the above

6. Which of these would *not* be a PR function?

   a. monitor and interpret events as they affect the organization
   b. define the organization's primary publics
   c. dictate to management which course of action to take
   d. evaluate the effectiveness of a PR campaign

7. All but one of the below are advantages of using an external PR firm; which *isn't* an advantage?

   a. most familiar with organization   c. most accessible
   b. least expensive to use   d. most objective

8. He was the first to put PR principles in writing with his 1923 book, *Crystallizing Public Opinion*.

   a. Ivy Lee   c. Edward L. Bernays
   b. George Parker   d. Carl Byoir

9. Which of these communication methods wouldn't a PR campaign use?

   a. mass media   c. interpersonal, machine assisted
   b. interpersonal   d. it might use all these methods

10. All but one of the below are advantages of using an external PR firm; which isn't?

    a. gives freshest approach to problem   c. least expensive to use
    b. has big assortment of media services   d. most objective in outlook

11. You would most likely see _____ plans in an organization's annual report.

    a. strategic   b. tactical

12. What's the best mass medium for reaching a PR target audience?

    a. television   c. interpersonal contacts
    b. newspapers   d. depends on the target public

13. In terms of a PR campaign, the department's main function would be to _____ the target public.

    a. inform   c. entertain
    b. distract   d. neutralize

14. From management's perspective, a PR director's principal role is that of:

    a. teacher   c. counselor
    b. decision maker   d. publicity generator

15. Which of these is *not* a reason for PR's growth since WWII?

    a. the rise of social responsibility as an organizational value
    b. growth of consumerism movement
    c. big increases in advertising budgets
    d. the need to identify and communicate with an organization's diverse publics

16. Techniques used to evaluate a PR campaign include all but:

    a. speculation   c. telephone surveys
    b. questionnaires   d. panel discussions or forums

17. "The situation isn't as bad as it looks." A comment like that would *most* likely come from a:

    a. press agent   c. publicist
    b. spin doctor   d. PR person

18. The director of PR usually reports directly to the:

    a. stockholders   c. company's CEO
    b. employees or union   d. marketing department

19. The management-by-objectives (MBO) approach to public relations allows a company to:

    a. evaluate a campaign's success   c. set specific, objective goals
    b. engage in long-term planning   d. all the above

20. External PR firms usually bill their clients in one of three ways: which of these doesn't belong?

    a. retainer fee   c. time and expenses
    b. fixed fees   d. by degree of campaign success

CHAPTER 16: TEST ANSWER KEYS

True/False Test

01. False	05. False	09. True	13. True
02. False	06. True	10. True	14. False
03. True	07. True	11. False	15. True
04. True	08. False	12. False	

Multiple-Choice Test

01. D	06. C	11. A	16. A
02. C	07. D	12. D	17. B
03. B	08. C	13. A	18. C
04. D	09. D	14. C	19. D
05. D	10. C	15. C	20. D

-------------- N O T E S --------------

Chapter 17

Structure of the Advertising Industry

This chapter surveys the "oil" that keeps the entire U.S. mass media system running: advertising, the consumer demands and the media revenue it generates. We'll see the ad industry from the inside out-- when it started and why; who makes ads and how; and who decides where they're placed and why.

CHAPTER OBJECTIVE

.   learn the individual roles and concerns of the ad industry's three main players: the advertisers themselves, the ad agency types, and how individual mass media are chosen as ad vehicles

KEY TERMS AND CONCEPTS

[ ]   advertising: (key definition terms: nonpersonal, paid for, identified sponsor)
[ ]   four basic functions advertising fulfills: (marketing; education; economics; social function)
[ ]   target audience: consumer advertising v. business-to-business advertising
[ ]   advertising's historical profile (especially role played by the industrial revolution)
[ ]   advertising agency ; [ ] Pure Food and Drug Act of 1906 (reasons and consequences)
[ ]   Federal Trade Commission (FTC) and its role with advertising
[ ]   advertising industry organization: (1) advertisers: national v. (local) retail, distinctions between; (2) agency types: *a.* full-service agency; *b.* media-buying service; *c.* creative boutique
[ ]   how each medium is evaluated for its advertising advantages or disadvantages:
    [ ] *reach:* how many people can get the message?
    [ ] *frequency:* how often will the message be received?
    [ ] *selectivity:* does the medium actually reach the "correct" audience?
    [ ] *efficiency:* what does it cost to reach a certain number of people (CPM, cost per thousand)
[ ]   typical ad agency organization:
    [ ] creative: produces ad copy (message, art work, scripting, arranges talent)
    [ ] account services: account executive (AE) serves as liaison between client and agency
    [ ] marketing services: advises which medium to use; also in charge of sales promotion items
    [ ] administration: management, business, and office functions
[ ]   ad campaign's steps: (1) choosing marketing strategy; (2) selecting theme; (3) translating theme into media types; (4) making ads; (5) buying space/time; (6) executing/evaluating campaign
[ ]   positioning; [ ] layouts; [ ] storyboard; [ ] economic profile of ad industry and related media
[ ]   ad agency compensation schemes: (1) media commissions; (2) agency charges; (3) retainer fees
[ ]   business-to-business advertising types: (1) trade; (2) industrial; (3) professional; (4) agricultural
[ ]   business v. consumer advertising, contrasts: (1) smaller target audiences; (2) technical, complex, high-priced products; (3) professional buyers; (4) personal sales approach; (5) distinct media mix
[ ]   current industry issues; (1) stimulates greed, envy, and avarice; (2) promotes materialistic values and lifestyles; (3) intrusiveness

TOPICS FOR DISCUSSION

1. Should any products or services be banned from being advertised on TV? Are there any legal products or services that you think shouldn't be allowed to be advertised in *any* medium?

2. Should advertisers be protected under the First Amendment's guarantees of free speech? If not, what limitations would you suggest?

3. Is it fair for big companies to express social or political views in advertisements when individual citizens can't afford to express counter ideas or compete with them on an equal footing?

4. Is it fair for advertisers to target children for products or services? Consider the recent charges that the tobacco industry deliberately targets children as potential buyers. At what age do you think children are capable enough to filter, interpret, and decide on the merits of an ad message?

5. Should advertising be allowed in schools? What about Channel One, whereby schools get huge material dividends (free TVS and programs in return for student exposure to Channel One ads)?

6. Ever notice that even though you paid for your car, you're the only one whose name isn't on it? Count how many organizations advertise on or in your car (dealer, manufacturer, associations, insurance companies, your workplace, city stickers, clubs, after-market sales, etc.) Assuming you care, what--if anything--could you do to curtail the practice?

7. Though most people complain about advertisements, they often do a remarkable job giving us new information and entertaining us. Make a quick list of five nontrivial things you've learned from ads. Describe your two favorite magazine and TV ads.

8. What type of ad do you think is most affective: those that annoy, startle, or excite you? Or what about ads that entertain you (humor, drama, mystery)? Or do the ads that appeal to your intellect work best? Explain and defend your answer.

9. Do you think being able to recall an advertisement equates to a successful ad? Have any ads (or spokespersons) annoyed you so much that you refuse to buy their product or service?

10. Government--from national departments to local villages--advertise for various reasons, usually informational. Where would you stop them in terms of what they shouldn't be allowed to say?

11. Why do public utilities like electric and gas companies advertise? What public service are they performing, or are they simply trying to generate good will at public expense?

12. Should TV infomercials be clearly labeled as sponsored advertisements instead of the talk-show programs they attempt to emulate?

13. Could you design an ad for this course? Should courses be advertised? Should college teachers be allowed to advertise? What people or organizations should or shouldn't? Why or why not?

Chapter 17: True/False Test

Structure of the Advertising Industry

1. Advertising was "invented" in America during colonial times.

2. The government began regulating the advertising industry with the introduction of the 1869 *Truth in Advertising* bill.

3. The Federal Communication Commission (FCC) regulates advertising.

4. A TV ad first takes shape in a rough draft called a *portfolio*.

5. An ad agency that concentrates on creating an advertising theme is called a creative boutique.

6. *Positioning* your product is the act of placing it relative to similar products, e.g., yours is the luxury version, the economy design, the longevity model, and so on.

7. Historically, ad agencies received a 15 percent rebate on the cost of ad space or time from the media in which the ads were placed; that practice, however, is now being augmented by newer compensation schemes.

8. Advertisements generally perform all four of the mass media functions, i.e., they educate, inform, persuade, and pass on our cultural values.

9. Media buying service agencies are really brokers, usually buying and selling ad space or time.

10. TV, though usually the most expensive medium, generally provides the lowest cost-per-thousand (CPM) in terms of ad efficiency.

11. Ads for a nuclear reactor would fall under the heading of *consumer* advertising.

12. The personal liaison between the ad agency and its client is called the *account executive*.

13. One of the big differences between consumer and business advertising target audiences is that the business audience tends to be a technically savvy, non-impulsive, cost-conscious professional.

14. The words or dialogue in an advertisement are called *copy*.

15. The *National Rifle Association Monthly* might be a good media vehicle for ad selectivity, but a poor one for ad frequency.

Chapter 17: Multiple-Choice Test

Structure of the Advertising Industry

1. As a rule, national advertising stresses:

   a. brand names and product features   c. prices
   b. local retail "sales"   d. location of product or service

2. The primary government overseer of the advertising industry is the:

   a. Federal Trade Commission   c. Federal Communications Commission
   b. Federal Drug Administration   d. Federal Board of Trade

3. Three of these items played a major role in first creating a national market for goods and services which, of course, helped create a need for national advertising. Which item doesn't belong?

   a. a steadily climbing population with increasing disposable income
   b. mass production
   c. a trans-continental railroad system
   d. national radio networks

4. Which medium usually achieves the biggest advertising *reach*?

   a. radio   c. newspapers
   b. television   d. magazines

5. Under normal circumstances, the best medium to assure the highest degree of target audience selectivity would be:

   a. radio   c. direct mail
   b. newspapers   d. magazines

6. Which type of advertising is *least* known to the general public?

   a. retail   c. point-of-purchase
   b. business-to-business   d. consumer

7. An ad's *efficiency* is usually measured in terms of:

    a. the cost per thousand (CPM) relative to the ad's target audience
    b. increase or decrease in point-of-purchase sales
    c. exit polls from sample stores and service centers
    d. Arbitron ratings

8. An ad agency's marketing department would perform all but which of these functions?

    a. determine the best media mix for the ad campaign
    b. evaluate the CPM efficiency for each medium
    c. create the ad campaign's main theme
    d. monitor or administer product promotions, such as coupons or premiums

9. A graphic outline of a proposed TV advertisement is called a:

    a. draft board   c. positioning board
    b. storyboard   d. campaign sketch

10. Which are the top two media in advertising sales revenue?

    a. TV and radio   c. newspapers and TV
    b. magazines and TV   d. TV and direct mail

11. Advertisers judge whether a medium is suitable for a particular ad campaign by evaluating that medium in four different ways; which of the below doesn't belong?

    a. reach   c. frequency
    b. efficiency   d. prestige value

12. If your ad campaign needs frequency, it's probably best to stay away from which medium?

    a. television   c. FM radio
    b. daily newspapers   d. magazines

13. Which of these statements is not generally true of advertising?

    a. ad claims are guaranteed by federal law   c. the source is identified
    b. it's a paid-for commodity   d. it's a nonpersonal communication vehicle

14. The significance of the *Pure Food and Drug Act* was that it was:

    a. the first federal law which attempted to control advertising
    b. the forerunner of the Federal Trade Commission
    c. the first attempt to self-regulate ad industry ethics
    d. conceived and promoted by the advertising industry itself

15. All but one of these mediums is a relatively new way to advertise; which one isn't?

    a. CD-ROM
    b. subliminal ads
    c. the Internet (on World Wide Web)
    d. computer disks

16. Advertising has drawn criticism since its inception. Your text cites three major areas with which critics have shown concern. Which item doesn't belong? Advertising:

    a. encourages materialism
    b. inspires greed, envy, and avarice
    c. promotes capitalism
    d. is too pervasive in our social environment

17. Identify the typically smaller target audience type for an ad campaign.

    a. business
    b. boutique
    c. consumer
    d. commissions

18. Which of the below isn't a major business-to-business advertising target:

    a. agriculture
    b. professional
    c. industrial
    d. individuals

19. When you *position* your product, you're:

    a. trying to show how well it works
    b. getting it ready for an ad campaign
    c. giving it a unique ad media mix
    d. positioning its features relative to similar products

20. Which medium below **best** fits the following ad vehicle profile for an all-Chicago target audience campaign? Low *reach*; good *frequency*; high *selectivity*; medium *efficiency*.

    a. a classical music FM radio station
    b. a large daily metro newspaper
    c. a monthly hobbyist magazine
    d. a network affiliate TV station

CHAPTER 17:   TEST ANSWER KEYS

True/False Test

01. False	05. True	09. True	13. True
02. False	06. True	10. True	14. True
03. False	07. True	11. False	15. True
04. False	08. True	12. True	

Multiple-Choice Test

01. A	06. B	11. D	16. C
02. A	07. A	12. D	17. A
03. D	08. C	13. A	18. D
04. B	09. B	14. A	19. D
05. C	10. C	15. B	20. A

-------------- **N O T E S** --------------

Chapter 18

Formal Controls: Laws, Rules, Regulations

In this chapter we explore the labyrinth of changing laws and rules that help shape what we can and cannot see or read in the media. We'll also look at how our country is striving to maintain traditional constitutional values in the face of a flurry of new mass media and our continuing cultural evolution.

CHAPTER OBJECTIVE

. come to an appreciation of the evolutionary nature of how and why we regulate mass media while noting continually changing current regulatory trends and the reasons for them

KEY TERMS AND CONCEPTS

[ ] First Amendment (freedoms and apparent limitations within)
[ ] prior restraint (*Near v. Minnesota,* Pentagon Papers, and Hazelwood cases); [ ] injunction
[ ] shield laws; [ ] reporter privilege, issues with; [ ] conflict between 1st and 6th Amendments
[ ] pretrial publicity, problems with; [ ] sequestering; [ ] moving trial location (change of venue:)
[ ] gag orders; [ ] press access to pretrial hearings, issues; [ ] secrecy of grand jury proceedings
[ ] Canon 35, circa 1930s; [ ] Canon 3A(7), circa 1972
[ ] Freedom of Information Act (FOIA, 1966); [ ] Sunshine Acts; [ ] press access to news events
[ ] defamation (reputation), types: [ ] libel; [ ] slander; [ ] libel per se; [ ] libel per quod
[ ] five elements needed to prove libel: (harm; identification; publication; media fault; falsity)
[ ] who has to prove what in libel cases; [ ] responsibility of media for the content it carries
[ ] libel defenses: truth; privilege; fair comment and criticism
[ ] *New York Times vs. Sullivan* case; [ ] actual malice; [ ] editorial advertising; [ ] damage types
[ ] invasion of privacy (peace of mind), types:
    [ ] intrusion (intruding upon a person's solitude or seclusion, cf. eavesdropping)
    [ ] unauthorized release of private information
    [ ] false light (creating false impressions)
    [ ] appropriation (of a person's name or likeness for commercial gain)
[ ] Copyright Act, 1976 (what's covered, what's not); [ ] length of copyright protection
[ ] fair use doctrine (factors: purpose of use, nature of work, amount reproduced, effect of use)
[ ] fair use doctrine (cf. "Betamax' case, issues surrounding)
[ ] obscenity and pornography (legal difficulties in defining abuses); [ ] indecent content
[ ] Hicklin Rule; [ ] *Roth vs. United* States; [ ] *Miller v. California* and later modifications
[ ] FCC's guidelines/powers: [ ] public interest; [ ] fines; [ ] license probation/suspension
[ ] FCC's content prohibitions, cf. the "raised eyebrow" warning technique
[ ] Children's TV Act; [ ] Equal Opportunities; [ ] Fairness Doctrine (in spirit, alive; in law, dead)
[ ] *Cable TV Act* of 1992, provisions of; [ ] franchises; [ ]commercial free speech, status of
[ ] FTC's legal guidelines and powers; [ ] consent orders; [ ] cease-and-desist orders

TOPICS FOR DISCUSSION

1. Doctors usually can't be required to testify in court about patients, or lawyers about clients, and priests about confessors. Is there a significant difference among these situations and journalists being required (in some states) to compromise their news sources?

2. The *Free Press v. Fair Trial* controversy is a battle between First and Sixth Amendment rights-- the public's right to know v. a defendant's right to a fair trial. Which right do you think is more important? Should we try to accommodate both rights?

3. Is it fair that a magazine or film be labeled pornographic in one town or state and not in another?

4. Are cameras allowed in courtrooms in your state? Do you think it's a good idea to have them there or not?

5. Obviously it's not a good idea for police to let just anyone visit a crime scene; but if reporters are serving as your representatives, shouldn't they be given special permission?

6. Why can't you libel a dead person? Can you sue for libel if what's been said about you simply hurts your feelings? Can you think of a situation where someone can be libeled per quod? Do you think you've ever been slandered (remember, malicious gossip is often slanderous).

7. Do you think the FCC is too strict, about right, or too loose in regulating broadcast content?

8. Is it fair that you can't photocopy a book for later reading or record a song off the air for later listening, but that you can videotape a TV program for later viewing?

9. Should advertisers have the same free speech guarantees you do?

10. Do you think your privacy has ever been invaded according to the "unauthorized-release-of-private-information" provisions of the privacy laws?

11. Do we really need anti-pornography laws (the protection of children, animals, and people who can't protect themselves being obvious exceptions)?

12. What information do you think the federal government might have on you? Where would you go to find out about if they did or not using the FOIA provisions? Do states have FOIAs?

13. Is your free speech violated if a judge issues a gag order stopping you from talking or writing about a pending case?

14. Not long ago a few reporters took to sifting through a person's garbage trying to uncover information. Do you think sifting through garbage is an invasion of your privacy? By police?

Chapter 18: True/False Test

Formal Controls: Laws, Rules, Regulations

1. The Supreme Court ruled that under certain rare circumstances, prior restraint is okay, i.e., the Court held that the First Amendment is not absolute; some press restrictions could apply.

2. If *you* sue a newspaper for libel, it's the newspaper that has to prove the story is true.

3. Shield laws are federal laws and therefore apply to all states.

4. Sunshine Acts, also known as *Open Meetings Acts*, ensure that, with some limitations, reporters and the public be allowed to observe government deliberations.

5. As the *Hicklin*, *Roth*, and *Miller* obscenity rulings attest, the main problem with regulating pornography and obscenity is that the terms defy precise, lasting, and universal definitions.

6. In the *Near v. Minnesota* case, the Supreme Court ruled that newspapers which are considered public nuisances or against the public interest can be shut down with a court-ordered injunction.

7. The Freedom of Information Act allows limited public access only to *federal* information.

8. A film, magazine, or TV program may have *indecent* content that isn't necessarily *pornographic*.

9. Today's court rulings suggest that the reporters have no more privileged right of access to news events or crime scenes than you do.

10. Libel is spoken defamation; slander is written.

11. The restrictions of Cannon 35 seem to be easing today, although only on a state-by-state basis.

12. In a libel suit, public officials or figures must prove something you don't need to: *actual malice*.

13. Legally, you commit video piracy by taping something off your television for later viewing.

14. Advertising and editorial material share equal protection under First Amendment guarantees.

15. Advertisers must have your consent to use your name, picture, or likeness in their ad.

Chapter 18: Multiple-Choice Test

Formal Controls: Laws, Rules, Regulations

1. Shield laws protect journalists from:

    a. judicial injunctions
    b. gag orders

    c. court-ordered subpoenas
    d. having to reveal their news sources

2. The Pentagon Papers case established:

    a. government can bring prior restraint cases to the courts to establish how much justification is needed to initiate action
    b. that basic First Amendment issues were posed, but not resolved
    c. there are no firm guidelines to the boundaries of press freedom
    d. all the above

3. Canon 35:

    a. is the only accepted 35-mm camera for courtroom photography
    b. was an American Bar Association advisory code (circa 1935) that effectively banned cameras and broadcast equipment in many state courtrooms for almost thirty years
    c. is a federal law banning TV coverage of criminal cases in federal courtrooms
    d. is none of the above

4. Find the false statement concerning current copyright laws?

    a. a copyright lasts for the life of the author plus fifty years
    b. to get a copyright, you need to register the work with the U.S. Register of Copyrights
    c. copyrightable items include ideas, procedures, and news
    d. it's okay to copy a part of a copyrighted work for educational or critique purposes

5. Which of these items *shouldn't* particularly interest the FCC when it comes time to renew a station's license?

    a. whether the broadcast content has been in the public interest
    b. the breadth of program diversity in the broadcast area
    c. cross ownership of media: what types and how many
    d. audience size and loyalty

6. Under well-defined conditions, the _____ protects people and companies from using bits and pieces of copyrighted material.

    a. duopoly rule
    b. fair use doctrine
    c. public interest doctrine
    d. Sunshine Act

7. Which of the following regulations is no longer in effect?

    a. Equal Opportunities Rule
    b. Freedom of Information Act
    c. Fairness Doctrine
    d. shield laws

8. The FTC regulates deceptive advertising. Which of these regulatory powers doesn't it have?

    a. collect fines
    b. issue cease-and-desist orders
    c. require corrective ads or proof of claims
    d. the FTC has all these powers

9. The FOIA isn't widely used by journalists because the:

    a. information received is generally dull
    b. processing costs are too expensive
    c. time it takes to get the information is too long
    d. restricted areas of information are so broad

10. This FCC rule tells stations to give opposing political candidates similar opportunities in terms of air time and costs.

    a. Fairness Doctrine
    b. Equal Opportunities rule
    c. Canon 35
    d. Betamax Doctrine

11. The _____ protect(s) people from having their photograph or name used for advertising purposes without their consent.

    a. Betamax Doctrine
    b. Hicklin Rule
    c. invasion of privacy laws
    d. Fairness Doctrine

12. In pornography cases the Supreme Court now suggests that this item should be considered the *prime* factor in determining guilt:

    a. whether isolated passages of the work are depraved
    b. whether it appeals to prurient interests
    c. whether it violates contemporary local standards
    d. whether the work is without utterly redeeming social value

13. This code sets *current* guideline standards for use of electronic equipment in courtrooms.

    a. Canon 35
    b. Canon 3A(7)

    c. sunshine laws
    d. fair use doctrine

14. Which of these factors *isn't* necessary in order for an *ordinary citizen* to prove libel?

    a. sufficient identification
    b. actual malice

    c. actual harm
    d. falsity

15. A judicial order that stops or prohibits someone from doing something is called:

    a. an injunction
    b. a gag order

    c. a subpoena
    d. sequestering

16. If you falsely write that you saw a pro-life advocate get an abortion, you are probably guilty of:

    a. slander
    b. libel per quod

    c. libel per se
    d. absolutely nothing

17. Which method wouldn't a judge use to protect a person's right to a fair and impartial trial?

    a. revoke station's license
    b. change the trial location

    c. gag order
    d. jury sequestering

18. Falsely write that someone is a thief or a liar, and you could be found guilty of:

    a. slander
    b. libel per quod

    c. libel per se
    d. false light

19. Which area is *least* protected under the Supreme Court's rules for First Amendment protection?

    a. high school newspapers
    b. advertisements

    c. music lyrics
    d. motion pictures

20. A gag order is normally issued by:

    a. a judge
    b. a district attorney

    c. an Appeals Court
    d. any legislative body

CHAPTER 18:   TEST ANSWER KEYS

True/False Test

01. True	05. True	09. True	13. False
02. False	06. False	10. False	14. False
03. False	07. True	11. True	15. True
04. True	08. True	12. True	

Multiple-Choice Test

01. D	06. B	11. C	16. B
02. D	07. C	12. C	17. A
03. B	08. D	13. B	18. C
04. C	09. C	14. B	19. A
05. D	10. B	15. A	20. A

-------------- N O T E S --------------

Chapter 19

Informal Controls: Ethics, Codes, Self-Regulations and External Pressures

We often think our conduct is limited only by our society's laws and rules; but we, and the media, are generally far more influenced by indirect guidelines and pressures, some stemming from the individual level, some from peer pressure, some from religious, political, or special-interest beliefs, and even from the business world. In this chapter we'll examine the tremendous influences on the media from these indirect sources--who does it, how it's done, and its ultimate effects.

CHAPTER OBJECTIVES

. appreciate the multitude of sources from and by which the media are controlled outside the realm of laws and regulations

. learn the basic tenets of the major Western ethical systems

. see how mass media guidelines attempt to balance freedom of expression with professional standards of conduct, and why and how those codes change over time

KEY TERMS AND CONCEPTS

[ ] personal ethics and ethical systems
   [ ] *Principle of the Golden Mean*, Aristotle (moral virtue lies between two extremes)
   [ ] *Categorical Imperative*, Immanuel Kant (what is right for one is right for all)
   [ ] *Principle of Utility* (utilitarianism), Mill and Bentham (greatest good for the greatest number)
   [ ] *Veil of Ignorance*, John Rawls (justice is blind)
   [ ] *Principle of self-determination*, Judeo-Christian (don't treat people as a means to an end)
   [ ] *Situational Ethics*, Joseph Fletcher (moral values vary from one situation to another)
[ ] model for making ethical decisions: *Definitions--->Values--->Principles--->Loyalties--->Action*
[ ] checkbook journalism; [ ] acculturation; [ ] performance codes of conduct (general definition)
[ ] prescriptive v. proscriptive ethical guidelines; [ ] media code enforceability, issues with
[ ] policy book, TV/radio; [ ] operating policies (internal) and editorial policies (external), print
[ ] boosterism; [ ] ombudsperson
[ ] outside influences: economics, pressure groups, press councils, and education

TOPICS FOR DISCUSSION

1. Is checkbook journalism ethical? What about "ambush" interviews? Or going "undercover?"

2. Have you disagreed with any media action in your region? Explain. What could you do, or did you do, to resolve the situation?

3. Given the six Western ethical systems outlined in this chapter, which comes closet to your own philosophy? Is yours a pure form or a combination of these systems? Do your classmates hold essentially similar positions or does the range of ethical stands vary greatly?

4. How can two people or groups agree on an ethical solution if their ideas are rooted within two different ethical foundations?

5. What pressure groups have you seen on campus, or in your home town, that tried to influence media performance? Do you think they succeeded? Do you think most groups speak for the majority of the population (consider the NRA, pro-life groups, ethnic and religious groups.).

6. If the media is governed by laws, and informally controlled by a host of pressure groups, is the same true for yourself as an individual? What pressure groups influence your behavior?

7. Is it a waste of effort for journalism to have codes of conduct if those codes remain unenforced?

8. Defend or attack this position: "The first rule of the media is to make money; ethical conduct is a by-product luxury. If they go bankrupt, then their ethical conduct is irrelevant."

9. CBS's *60 Minutes* and other news programs are often targeted by people who criticize how news is obtained, even if the end result is beneficial. The old issue of, "Do the means justify the end?" remains. How might each of the six ethical systems cited in your text address that issue?

10. Is it ethical for a photographer to cover a disaster rather than get personally involved (assuming that could be useful), or should his loyalty lie with the general public need to be informed?

11. Which is ethically worse: sins of commission or omission--or are they equally harmful?

12. Many critics suggest that America is going through an era of ethical crisis--not only in the mass media, but also in business, medicine, politics, law, religion, and so on. But are we? If so, is the general situation getting better or worse? Explain.

13. If a situation can have multiple ethical solutions (and thereby multiple outcomes), why not work backwards? Pick the outcome you want and then find the ethical system that justifies it. Can a solution be ethical but not the approach to it?

14. Can you think of any situation that would have a "no win" ethical solution?

Chapter 19: True/False Test

Informal Controls: Ethics, Codes, Self-Regulations and External Pressures

1. *Ethics* are the philosophical guidelines to understanding God, beauty, and the universe.

2. The ethical systems depicted in the text are products of Western thinking, i.e., they don't show how a Hindu, Muslim, Buddhist, or Eastern philosophy would handle ethical problems.

3. Applying ethical rules universally (what's right for one is right for all) indicates you're following Immanuel Kant's "Categorical Imperative."

4. Doing "all things in moderation" suggests you believe in Aristotle's system of the Golden Mean.

5. In *Star Trek II, The Wrath of Khan,* Spock dies while uttering the idea that the "good of the many outweigh the good of the one." That philosophy reflects the principles of utilitarianism.

6. Acculturation is synonymous with losing your objectivity.

7. Media codes of conduct apply only to news operations, not entertainment or advertising.

8. To get a film booked into a theater, producers *must* submit their films for an MPAA rating.

9. Most media codes are toothless, that is, they carry no penalties.

10. A *proscriptive* code tells you what *not* to do.

11. Program censorship at TV networks is basically nonexistent today.

12. An *ombudsperson* is the executive in charge of filtering media content, news or entertainment.

13. Where a paper stands on local issues can most likely be found in its operating policies manual.

14. Most media code violations are also federal or state legal violations.

15. Laws are to "must do" what ethics are to "should do."

Chapter 19: Multiple-Choice Test

Informal Controls: Ethics, Codes, Self-Regulations and External Pressures

1. *Scenario:* Your newspaper is criticized for its in-depth coverage of everything about the private lives of the political candidates currently running for office in your town. Reacting to pressure, your editor now orders that nothing be said about their private lives. Then new criticism comes in that your paper is too easy on them and that you're covering up for the candidates.

   The editor suggests a new and more moderate approach, i.e., that coverage of candidates' private lives be limited to revelations that only have bearing on their ability to carry out the duties of the offices they're seeking. This *compromise* position suggests an ethical solution closest to:

   a. Aristotle's golden mean   c. the categorical imperative
   b. situational ethics   d. utilitarianism

2. Someone who subscribes to the belief that ethical dilemmas must be solved on a case-by-case basis is most closely aligned with which of the below principles?

   a. the golden mean   c. situational ethics
   b. utilitarianism   d. self-determination

3. The ethical system that is unconditional, allowing no exceptions or extenuating circumstances is:

   a. Judeo-Christian ethics   c. categorical imperative
   b. utilitarianism   d. veil of ignorance

4. A major difference between many professional codes of conduct (medicine, law, education) and those in the mass media is that media codes:

   a. are strictly enforced   c. are reviewed by boards with punitive powers
   b. usually carry no sanctions   d. are universally followed

5. Which of the below would not be a factor in determining a course of individual action when faced with an ethical dilemma?

   a. define the situation and understand the values involved
   b. determine where your primary loyalties lie
   c. determine the ethical principles at issue
   d. arrive at a compromise with the individuals involved

6. *Scenario:* As president of a giant music distributing company, you decide to treat all radio stations--big and small--equally, feeling that "What's fair for one is fair for all." Your action suggests you're following which of the following ethical systems?

    a. the categorical imperative   c. self-determination
    b. utilitarianism   d. the golden mean

7. In researching job efficiency you discover that men who exercise seem better at detail work than men who don't exercise. But in your report you simply state that some men seem better at detail work than others. This suggests you're following which ethical system?

    a. veil of ignorance   c. self-determination
    b. utilitarianism   d. situation ethics

8. Using a news informant on an expendable basis is a violation of which ethical principle?

    a. veil of ignorance   c. self-determination
    b. utilitarianism   d. situation ethics

9. *Acculturation* happens to reporters when they:

    a. adopt the values of groups they cover   c. adhere to only one ethical system
    b. cover different cultures other than theirs d. become calloused over the issues they cover

10. Which film category has declined the most under the MPAA code?

    a. PG-13   c. G
    b. NC-17   d. R

11. Who's responsible for making the movie rating system work?

    a. film audiences   c. theater owners
    b. producers   d. all the above

12. Some TV stations have begun to run ads for condoms. Acknowledging that a few people may find these ads offensive, the stations counter that the ads are being run on the basis of doing the greatest good for the greatest number for their audience. This approach relates most closely to:

    a. the golden mean   c. categorical imperative
    b. utilitarianism   d. veil of ignorance

13. A prescriptive policy book would:

    a. tell you what to do
    b. outline possible penalties

    c. tell you what not to do
    d. none of the above

14. A newspaper's pro-choice or pro-life stand reflects its:

    a. policy book
    b. professional code

    c. operating policy
    d. editorial policy

15. Assuming your newspaper had one, a reader would go to this person with a complaint.

    a. code enforcer
    b. ombudsperson

    c. editorial board
    d. news review council

16. Which of these groups would probably exert the *least* pressure on the media?

    a. athletes
    b. special-interest groups

    c. advertisers
    d. religious and ethnic groups

17. "Boosterism" is similar in effect or intention to:

    a. libertarianism
    b. social responsibility

    c. developmental journalism
    d. checkbook journalism

18. Which of these media is the *least* likely to suffer pressure from advertiser pressure?

    a. newspapers
    b. cable networks

    c. television
    d. film industry

19. Which of these isn't a typical source of *informal* media control?

    a. pressure groups
    b. FCC

    c. press councils
    d. educational institutions

20. Three items below are typical of the *outside* forces that influence the mass media; which isn't?

    a. pressure groups
    b. economics

    c. press councils
    d. ombudsperson

CHAPTER 19: TEST ANSWER KEYS

True/False Test

01. False	05. True	09. True	13. False
02. True	06. True	10. True	14. False
03. True	07. False	11. True	15. True
04. True	08. False	12. False	

Multiple-Choice Test

01. A	06. A	11. D	16. A
02. C	07. A	12. B	17. C
03. C	08. C	13. A	18. D
04. B	09. A	14. D	19. B
05. D	10. C	15. B	20. D

-------------- N O T E S --------------

Chapter 20

Audience Characteristics and Patterns of Use

What we know about individual audiences of mass media is little; taken on the aggregate level however, we can see definite and consistent patterns of usage in terms of age, income, education, geography, and gender. This chapter shows what we know about these patterns for each of the mass media; we'll see how each medium passes through, or heads toward, four specific audience patterns. We'll see how these patterns change as both individual consumers and individual media evolve.

CHAPTER OBJECTIVES

. learn the four stages of a medium's general audience evolution

. come to understand the general usage patterns for each mass media

KEY TERMS AND CONCEPTS

[ ] stages of audience evolution
    [ ] elite stage (small, highly educated group)
    [ ] mass stage (the entire population)
    [ ] specialized stage (fragmented, special-interest groups)
    [ ] interactive stage (audience member exercises some control over media content and delivery)
[ ] influencing factors of audience evolution: social/educational/leisure; technological; economical
[ ] print media audiences, characteristics of (still primarily in specialized stage)
[ ] radio and recording audiences, characteristics of (still primarily in specialized stage}
[ ] film and TV audiences, characteristics of (still primarily in specialized stage}

NOTE: For statistical profiles of audiences, the primary thing to remember is general trends, main ideas, and significant numbers rather than every date, amount, or figure in a table or chart.

[ ] mass media audiences, characteristics and profiles of:
    [ ] newspapers;   [ ] magazines;   [ ] books;   [ ] radio;   [ ] music;   [ ] film;   [ ] television
[ ] relationship between age and media usage (how aging changes everything)
[ ] multistep flow model of media influence (most influence comes through nearby opinion leaders)

TOPICS FOR DISCUSSION

1. The audience patterns cited in the text are for the hypothetical "average" user; most people, of course, will fall in ranges above or below the averages. How do *you* fit relative to each medium's average? Using the chart on page 489 and the *average* user statistics for each medium, draw up a composite profile of yourself compared to the average person for each medium. What about your class? Taken as a whole, does it better begin to fit the *average* media user statistics?

2. Which medium's audience pattern do you find most difficult to believe? Why?

3. Travel to the future: describe how each medium might become totally interactive. Speculate on what each could be like. Be creative (you'll probably fall short of what will happen anyway).

4. Why is there a drop in media usage at age 65? As our life expectancy increases, do you believe that media usage will drop, remain stable, or climb?

5. A person's degree of wealth has a direct and consistent relationship to print media usage. Do the rich get richer because of print media? If so, what is it that print media provides these people to make increased wealth almost a statistical certainty?

6. It's a common complaint that kids watch too much TV; however, the chart on page 489 clearly shows that they watch far less TV than older people, and that in fact we watch more TV as we grow older. Do you think we're simply unaware of how much time we ourselves watch TV?

7. Why is "going to the show" primarily an under-25 experience? What do you think makes going out to a theater less appealing the older we get?

8. One way CDs are becoming interactive (see item 3 above) is that a few companies now allow you to check off the songs you want on a CD. In return, you get a custom-made CD with just the songs you want (currently using only recordings that are at least ten years old). Prices are higher than average, but the results are more selective. Would you be a potential customer?

9. What do you think about books, films, and TV programs where you help determine the ending? Wouldn't knowing what's going to happen (or likely to happen) be dull?

10. Do you see a danger in our society developing into media "haves" and "have nots" in terms of affordability? What happens when only wealthier Americans can afford access to the best media or the most productive information? Wouldn't that situation help contribute to a hardening of our economic class strata?

11. The more leisure time you have and the more disposable income you acquire, the more you can spend of both on the media. Has that been true for you?

12. Have you every been to a *Rocky Horror Picture Show*? If so, describe the experience.

139

Chapter 20:   True/False Test

Audience Characteristics and Patterns of Use

1. Most movie goers are under 30 years old.

2. Age doesn't play an important determining factor in which media we use or how we use it.

3. Each mass medium has now reached, and in various ways is deeply engaged in, the fourth stage of audience evolution: *audience interaction.*

4. Mass media fragmentation is really a reflection of the media catering to specialized audiences.

5. Of all media, the film and recording industries know the least facts about their customers.

6. The majority of newspapers and magazines are purchased on impulse from newsstands.

7. The "typical" book reader is a college-educated female, 35-49.

8. The more a medium relies on ad revenue (versus point-of-purchase sales) the more we know about its audience demographics.

9. The older you get, the more likely you are to evolve out of one audience format to another.

10. Perhaps the most common denominator of a print media consumer is his or her educational level.

11. The *multistep flow model* suggests that the mass media alone is unlikely to change your opinion on important issues; instead, this theory suggests, your views will most likely follow the opinion leaders in your own particular social group.

12. The *interactive* audience stage suggests an audience that has some selective control over a medium's content and form.

13. Almost every medium now has some form of interactivity.

14. *The Rocky Horror Picture Show* best exemplifies an *elitist* audience.

15. A medium's overall audience tends to evolve through four stages; however, a medium can still retain remnants of all its early stages as it continues to mature.

Chapter 20: Multiple Choice Test

Audience Characteristics and Patterns of Use

1. What stage of audience evolution usually comes first?

   a. elite
   b. mass

   c. specialized
   d. interactive

2. In what audience stage does the audience exercise the greatest control over the media?

   a. elite
   b. mass

   c. specialized
   d. interactive

3. Today's print media audiences tend to be mostly in what audience stage?

   a. elite
   b. mass

   c. specialized
   d. interactive

4. A call-in talk-radio format reflects what kind of audience?

   a. elite
   b. mass

   c. specialized
   d. interactive

5. What medium essentially went directly to the *mass* audience stage?

   a. books
   b. magazines

   c. film
   d. newspapers

6. Which of these is *not* a true reflection of newspapers today?

   a. daily circulation hasn't changed much in twenty-five years or so
   b. weekly newspaper readership continues to increase
   c. fewer people read papers relative to the increase in population
   d. more poor people read newspapers now than ever before

7. _____ have avoided a drop in audience levels primarily through continuing specialization

   a. Newspapers
   b. Magazines

   c. Books
   d. all the above

8. Which media pair below represents the *most* highly specialized (or fragmented) audiences?

   a. AM radio and newspapers
   b. magazines and FM radio

   c. recording and film
   d. broadcast TV and books

9. The older we get, the more likely we are to use this medium:

   a. theater films
   b. FM radio

   c. newspapers
   d. television

10. Which media pair below do we know the *least* about in terms of audience demographics?

    a. AM radio and newspapers
    b. magazines and FM radio

    c. recording and film
    d. television and books

11. On average, TV is on about _____ a day, with each of us watching for about _____ a day.

    a. 3 hours and 1 hour
    b. 5 hours and 2 hours

    c. 7 hours and 3 hours
    d. 9 hours and 4 hours

12. Most Americans now get their news from which medium?

    a. television
    b. radio

    c. newspapers
    d. magazines

13. Most VCR playback time (about 3/4) is used to watch:

    a. soap operas
    b. prime-time shows

    c. rented or purchased tapes
    d. homemade videos

14. From which medium do most of us now get their news, and which medium do we trust most?

    a. television
    b. radio

    c. newspapers
    d. magazines

15. Which of the below demographic profiles *doesn't* fit the average TV audience?

    a. low-income families watch more TV than middle-income families
    b. the higher your educational level, the less you tend to watch TV
    c. cable subscribers are older, have fewer children, and are less affluent than average
    d. teenagers watch the least of all major audience categories

16. The older we get, we dramatically lose the *most* interest in which medium?

    a. theater films   c. newspapers
    b. FM radio   d. television

17. In which audience stage would a mass medium most likely be catering to the least common denominator of audience tastes?

    a. elite   c. specialized
    b. mass   d. interactive

18. Print media is flirting with interactivity via which of the following methods?

    a. telephones   c. online bulletin boards
    b. fax machines   d. all the above

19. Which is a *false* statement about the average magazine reader or the magazine industry?

    a. most readers buy their magazines at newsstands
    b. readership continues to rise per 1000 people
    c. audiences have become increasingly specialized
    d. readers tend to be better educated, be "joiners," and more likely to belong to organizations

20. Which is a *false* statement about the average radio listener or the radio industry?

    a. there are about twice as many radios in this country as people
    b. the average person will have his or her radio on about three hours per day
    c. AM listenership is now about equal with FM
    d. listeners "evolve" from one radio format to another as they grow older

CHAPTER 20: TEST ANSWER KEYS

True/False Test

01. True	05. True	09. True	13. True
02. False	06. False	10. True	14. False
03. False	07. True	11. True	15. True
04. True	08. True	12. True	

Multiple-Choice Test

01. A	06. D	11. C	16. A
02. D	07. D	12. A	17. B
03. C	08. B	13. C	18. D
04. D	09. D	14. A	19. A
05. C	10. C	15. C	20. C

-------------- **N O T E S** --------------

Chapter 21

Mass Media Feedback Systems

In this chapter we see how the media answers the question, "How are we doing?" Sometimes answers spring spontaneously from the audiences; but for bench mark, profit-tabulating figures, the media usually relies on expensive and sophisticated polling systems. We'll examine these systems on a medium-by-medium basis, finding out who measures what, when, and how.

CHAPTER OBJECTIVES

.   see the qualitative and quantitative differences between audience and media-generated feedback

.   learn how to calculate ratings and shares; understand how polls work

KEY TERMS AND CONCEPTS

[ ] audience-generated v. media-originated feedback, characteristics of (see table on text p. 498)
[ ] quantitative media-feedback sources:
    [ ] A.C. Nielsen (TV);   [ ] Arbitron (radio);   [ ] Audit Bureau of Circulation (newspapers)
    [ ] *Variety* (movies);   [ ] *Billboard* (music); [ ] *Publishers Weekly/New York Times* (books)
    [ ] *Simmons Market Research Bureau* and *Mediamark* (magazines)
        [ ] magazine audience types: primary v. pass-along, profiles of
[ ] qualitative audience-feedback sources: letters-to-the-editor; call-ins; petition campaigns; online responses, FCC's *Petition to Deny* (license renewal), characteristics of all feedback forms
[ ] feedback: television and film
    [ ] Nielsen's *Peoplemeter*: what it measures and how
    [ ] population; [ ] sample; [ ] sampling error
    [ ] local-market TV rating systems
    [ ] *ratings*   = # of households watching a program / # of TV households
    [ ] *shares*   = # of households watching a program / # households using (watching) TV
[ ] *sweep* period; [ ] concept testing; [ ] pilot testing; [ ] focus group (film)

TOPICS FOR DISCUSSION

1. How much faith do you put in the rating system for *any* medium?

2. Do you think rating systems are somewhat self-fulfilling, i.e., success breeds success or failure breeds failure? For example, if a film makes a big hit its first week out, other people may think its so good that they want to see it too, thereby making weeks two, three, and so on a success.

3. Have you ever encountered a top-rated song, book, TV program, or film and wondered why so many people apparently thought it was good (when you thought just the opposite)?

4. Almost everyone in college has either written a letter to a newspaper or magazine, called a radio station, or been involved in a media poll. Share your experiences and impressions.

5. Have you, or anyone you know, ever been successful in changing a medium's content? Have you ever been part of a special-interest group trying to accomplish similar ends with a petition drive?

6. How should the media react to pressure from special-interest groups? Is such pressure equitable, considering the group probably doesn't accurately represent the audience as a whole?

7. If the media continues to pattern its content to what audiences want, won't media creativity and autonomy dry up?

8. How much do you rely on media lists for your own personal media consumption, i.e., Top-10 books, Top-40 songs, top box office films, high-ratings TV programs, and so on?

9. How well do media critics do in predicting *your* tastes?

10. Say you wanted to mount a campaign against a particular medium outlet (we're not encouraging that you do); how would you do it? Are there ethical issues involved? What about the economic fallout (will someone suffer)? For example, several movie theater chains now show commercials before a film. If you don't like the idea (and who does?), how might you go about changing the theater owner's mind? The advertiser's? The film distributor's?

11. Whatever the current month now, a February, May, July, or November *sweep week* should be coming up soon. During these times some local TV stations hype their news shows to tease and attract more viewers. What are your views on the propriety of hyping news shows (to get better ratings) by featuring sensationalistic feature stories?

12. Here's a *very* creative challenge: Can you think of an inexpensive rival to the "Van Dorps" TV rating system?

Chapter 21: True/False Test

Mass Media Feedback Systems

1. Most audience-driven feedback is delayed and indirect.

2. TV audience feedback is more influential in altering programming than media-originated types.

3. People who write to a TV network tend to reflect the feelings of the general population.

4. *Quantitative* feedback deals with numbers, e.g., statistics, ratings, and shares.

5. Audience-generated feedback is usually opinion oriented, i.e., a *qualitative* response.

6. If you wanted the FCC to deny a radio station's license at renewal time, you'll need to submit an official *Petition to Deny* form.

7. *Billboard* determines the *Hot-100 Chart* by polling the leading recording *studios* each week.

8. TV gets more audience letters than newspapers, mostly due to special-interest letter campaigns.

9. A *sweep period* is a time wherein a TV station wins five or more of the Top-10 program spots.

10. *Ratings* measure a show's popularity relative to other shows airing at the same time; that is, ratings = the # of households watching a program divided by the # of households watching TV.

11. Polling 200 out of 10,000 people gives you essentially the same degree of sampling error as polling 200 people out of 10,000,000.

12. The larger a poll's sample size, the smaller the sampling error.

13. Arbitron rates local radio stations.

14. People involved in a *concept test* or *pilot test* are reacting to proposed *movie* ideas.

15. A *focus group* could change a film's ending or plot.

Chapter 21: Multiple-Choice Test

Mass Media Feedback Systems

1. Compared to the general audience, people who write letters to the media tend to fall into three of the below categories. Which profile doesn't fit? Letter writers are:

   a. older
   b. wealthier

   c. better educated professionals
   d. younger

2. Match the feedback pattern below with correct feedback source.

   - generally not typical of entire audience
   - opinions expressed qualitatively
   - individuals determine feedback's form and channel

   a. audience-generated

   b. media-originated

3. Which medium is *least* likely to know very much about the demographics of its audience?

   a. magazines
   b. film

   c. FM
   d. TV

4. One of the methods Arbitron uses to rate radio stations is by asking selected listeners to use a:

   a. diary
   b. peoplemeter

   c. special radio
   d. none of the above

5. To decrease sampling error, increase:

   a. population size
   b. sample size

   c. audience selectivity
   d. polling frequency

6. Turn to *Variety* for the latest _____ industry news and statistics.

   a. TV
   b. radio

   c. music
   d. film

7. Which of these statements is *not* true concerning the Audit Bureau of Circulation?

    a. does on-site audits of subscription and newsstand sales records
    b. its services are funded by member dues and service fees
    c. its purpose is to independently insure the accuracy of newspaper circulation figures
    d. ABC members are audited only once every ten years

8. Check here for the current best-selling books:

    a. *Billboard*   c. *Folio*
    b. *Variety*   d. *Publishers Weekly* or the *New York Times*

9. Find the *rating* for WLS-TV.   **Data:** (1) market size = 10,000,000; (2) HUT (homes using TV) = 2,500,000; (3) # of people watching WLS-TV = 250,000

    a. 2.5   c. 25.0
    b. 10.0   d. none of the above

10. Find the *share* for WLS-TV.   **Data:** (1) market size = 10,000,000; (2) HUT (homes using TV) = 2,500,000; (3) # of people watching WLS-TV = 250,000

    a. 2.5   c. 25.0
    b. 10.0   d. none of the above

11. How many people are watching WBBM-TV based on the following data. (1) market size = 10,000,000; (2) HUT (homes using TV) = 2,000,000; (3) WBBM's rating = 15; share = 75

    a. 150,000   c. 1,500,000
    b. 300,000   d. 7,500,000

12. The first actually produced episode of a proposed TV series is called a:

    a. demo   c. pilot
    b. sample   d. concept test

13. In determining how much to charge for advertising space, most magazines base their rates on data received from:

    a. *Publisher's Weekly*   c. Starch Reports
    b. A. C. Nielsen   d. Simmons Market Research Bureau or Mediamark

14. Which of the below would have the *least* effect on changing a TV network's mind to cancel a popular program series?

    a. ratings
    b. 3000 thoughtful letters

    c. 30,000 letters from a special-interest campaign
    d. shares

15. Ratings and shares are examples of:

    a. qualitative, media-originated feedback
    b. quantitative, media-originated feedback

    c. qualitative, audience-generated feedback
    d. quantitative, audience-generated feedback

16. Initial film "ratings" are measured in terms of:

    a. box office receipts
    b. film rental receipts

    c. Pay Per View requests
    d. a *Billboard* poll

17. Find the false statement concerning the *Peoplemeter* system:

    a. tracks programs watched by individual household members
    b. checks people with hidden cameras, matching their image against a computer-stored image
    c. population sample changed every two years
    d. expensive procedure; used in 4000 households nationally; data downloaded to A.C. Nielsen

18. Because of the nature of this particular feedback medium, TV producers would probably give the *most* attention to audience opinions expressed through:

    a. e-mail or online discussion groups
    b. campaign letters

    c. phone calls
    d. professional program critics

19. Which of the following doesn't fit the general profile of media-originated feedback?

    a. gathered by a third party
    b. delayed

    c. examines a representative audience cross section
    d. expressed qualitatively

20. Which of the following doesn't fit the general profile of audience-originated feedback?

    a. audience determines form and channel
    b. expressed quantitatively

    c. generally not typical of entire audience
    d. travels directly to a media organization

CHAPTER 21: TEST ANSWER KEYS

True/False Test

01. True	05. True	09. False	13. True
02. False	06. True	10. False	14. False
03. False	07. False	11. True	15. True
04. True	08. True	12. True	

Multiple-Choice Test

01. D	06. D	11. C	16. A
02. A	07. D	12. C	17. B
03. B	08. D	13. D	18. A
04. A	09. A	14. C	19. D
05. B	10. B	15. B	20. B

-------------- **N O T E S** --------------

Chapter 22

Effects of Mass Communication on Knowledge and Attitudes

What we know about our world, how we perceive and behave in it, and our attitudes toward it are influenced primarily by the people around us. What role the media plays in influencing us is still in question, but that it does (to some degree) is relatively certain. The primary questions seem to be: "At what times, for how long, to what degree, and to what effect (good or bad) does the mass media influence our collective attitudes, knowledge, and perceptions?"

CHAPTER OBJECTIVES

- learn the various sources through which people, especially children, are "socialized" within their world and the role that the mass media seem to play in this process

- study the phenomenon of cultivation analysis to see how TV may alter the way people perceive their world, especially heavy TV users

- understand the process and significance of the mass media's agenda setting function

KEY TERMS AND CONCEPTS

[ ] socialization (see also Chapter 2); [ ] agencies (sources) of socialization
[ ] observational learning (cf. formal training or direct experience)
[ ] television as the media's primary news and information delivery source
[ ] three factors that make TV an influential force with children: (1) stereotyping (ideas, people, and behaviors); (2) heavy TV exposure; (3) no alternative set of beliefs
[ ] cultivation analysis (promotes perceptions of reality consistent with the way the world is presented in TV programs; approach concentrates primarily on long-term effects)
[ ] three problems that plague the accuracy of cultivation analysis: (1) difficult to determine cause and effect; (2) TV viewers differ in other ways than just their TV viewing patterns; (3) technical decisions on how TV viewing and attitudes are measured can significantly influence the findings.
[ ] mainstreaming; [ ] resonance
[ ] Three reasons why children are a special TV audience in terms of advertising: (1) vulnerability; (2) easily deceived; (3) potential socialization effects on them as future consumers
[ ] agenda setting, characteristics of; [ ] framing; [ ] agenda building

TOPICS FOR DISCUSSION

1. Do you think TV (or for that matter, *any* medium) is, in any significant way, responsible for making you the person you are today?

2. Are children growing up too quickly? Explain. Do you see any possibility that society can ever again create a "kids only" environment? Or was there ever such a place or time?

3. Describe someone you know who you'd say is a heavy TV user (by the way, would they agree with your appraisal?). Does he/she fit the behavioral or attitudinal patterns outlined in the text?

4. Make a list--in a descending order--of the five most important people or sources from which you acquired your most meaningful attitudes toward, and knowledge of, the world. Do you thing your list would change--in either content or order--depending on at what age you made it out?

5. From what primary source do your knowledge and attitudes stem concerning such things as: Bosnia? Congressional leaders? Life in China? Compare that knowledge base with what you know about local political leaders, local entertainment hot spots, or problems at your local high school. What conclusions might you draw from your assessment?

6. Make a list--in a descending order of importance--of the five most irksome TV stereotypes.

7. Now make a list--in a descending order of importance--of the five most accurate TV stereotypes, or is that in itself an oxymoron?

8. Do you think you've ever experienced any *negative* socialization or cultivational TV effects?

9. Can you think of any short-term effects (good or bad) that TV programs have ever had on you? What about long-term effects?

10. Name three subjects for which TV is absolutely your only source of information?

11. The more important something is to you, the less likely you are to rely on a single source of information about that topic. Try this: From how many sources do you get information about relationships? Worthwhile movies? Your favorite hobby? Sports? Fashion tips?

12. Do you think the media has *cultivated* any of your significant and lasting attitudes or behaviors?

13. By the time children reach the age of 15, the credibility they give to advertising "honesty" has dropped to about five percent (from a high of thirty-five percent at age 5-7). What "honesty " percentage would you now award TV ads?

14. Do you believe advertising creates a lasting sense of materialism in people, or is "wanting things" just a part of the human condition?

Chapter 22: True/False Test

Effects of Mass Communication on Knowledge and Attitudes

1. One media observer has suggested that, "The media may not always be successful in telling us what to think, but they are usually successful in telling us what to think about."

2. Film is the medium with the biggest potential for transmitting knowledge and beliefs between groups, and it is particularly influential in the socialization of children.

3. The socialization process happens quickly, and usually from only one main source.

4. Children can't learn good behavior from *fictional* characters.

5. Lacking guidance from any other source, a child is likely to adopt the TV version of a fact or situation as "true."

6. *Cultivation analysis* suggests that TV may cultivate a perception of the world *inconsistent* with the facts and circumstances of the "real" world.

7. After extensive research, scholars have finally proven a definite cause-and-effect relationship between positive TV roles and positive behavior in children.

8. Our perceived significance of a topic often depends on how much coverage it gets in the media.

9. Some critics suggest that advertising , in its long-term effects, actually fosters anti-materialism..

10. The ability to distinguish commercials from regular programming seems directly related to audience age, i.e, the younger the audience, the less discrimination they seem to exercise.

11. Apparently the cultivation effect is more complex than originally thought, e.g., both the type of TV content seen and a "time dissipation impact" seems to influence the cultivation effect.

12. Researchers have found no conclusive evidence of positive effects coming from TV programs.

13. TV effectively avoids stereotyping people since it routinely presents images that parallel reality.

14. Newspapers are most often cited as the public's biggest source of news and information.

15. Researchers suggest that the way an item is framed, i.e., how a topic or issue is presented in the media, has a direct bearing on how the public comes to view its significance, or even the attitude we collectively might take towards that topic. That process is called *framing*.

Chapter 22: Multiple-Choice Test

Effects of Mass Communication on Knowledge and Attitudes

1. The _____ industry has the greatest potential for socialization impact, especially with children.

   a. music
   b. film
   c. TV
   d. print

2. Children mainly acquire attitudes, knowledge, and learn behavior from all these sources except:

   a. formal instruction
   b. direct experience
   c. observational learning
   d. intuition

3. Researchers find that children's TV programs can impart all but:

   a. information
   b. skills
   c. attitudes
   d. they can impart all the above

4. Cultivation analysis deals *least* with the following:

   a how we determine what is currently an important public issue
   b. how the media may shape the way we perceive our world
   c. the "real" world v. the world portrayed by the media
   d. long-term media effects on personal attitudes and behavior patterns

5. Cultivation analysis suffers from three major problems; which of these isn't one of them?

   a. young men react to TV content very differently than women
   b. it's hard to find cause-and-effect relationships between the amount and content of TV viewing
   c. TV viewers may differ in significant ways other than in which shows they watch or how many
   d. technical decisions about the way TV viewing and attitudes are measured can have a significant impact on research findings

6. Cultivation analysis research says that a distorted view of reality would *most likely* be held by:

   a. heavy TV viewers
   b. the very rich
   c. the better educated
   d. teenagers

7. In terms of advertising, which of these *doesn't* isolate children as a special type of TV audience?

    a. they're protected from exploitation by the National Advertising Council's Code of Conduct
    b. their own vulnerability, i.e., a conceptual naivete about advertising's role and function
    c. easily deceived by special effects
    d. potential advertising socialization could adversely affect them as future consumers

8. Concerning TV ads, which of these effects does *not* happen to children as they grow older?

    a. parental consumer influence drops, peer influence rises
    b. advertising naivete generally decreases
    c. distrust of commercials rises
    d. ability to distinguish between what a *necessity* is and what a *luxury* is diminishes

9. _____ reflects the idea that the press confers importance on an event simply by reporting it.

    a. Saturation   c. Gatekeeping
    b. Cultivation   d. Agenda setting

10. Research suggests that this medium has the greatest influence in setting the public agenda?

    a. books   c. newspapers
    b. TV   d. magazines

11. Studies suggest that children who are exposed to repeated episodes of TV violence:

    a. become more fearful of the world   c. see the world as more dangerous than it really is
    b. can become calloused to violence   d. all the above

12. Mass media research in cultivational analysis:

    a. absolutely proves that mass media plays a critical role in creating attitudes
    b. only suggests associations between heavy TV use and attitudes
    c. confirms definite cause-and-effect relationships
    d. clearly establishes a reciprocal causation between heavy TV use and attitude formation

13. Which of the below groups do TV programs consistently and seriously overrepresent?

    a. lawyers   c. doctors and nurses
    b. police agents   d. journalists

14 Knowledge, values, and attitudes can be acquired from:

a. TV
b. music
c. films
d. all the above

15. The most likely time the media has the biggest socialization effect on children's attitudes is when:

a. they are between 12-16 years old
b. there is no alternative set of beliefs
c. the program presents highly dramatic action
d. they come from a divorced family

16. TV can be a big influence in forming children's attitudes when all but which of these is present?

a. stereotypes are constantly portrayed
b. there is no alternative set of beliefs
c. the children in question are heavy TV watchers
d. conflicts exist between TV *reality* and their own

17. Which of the below is the least likely to be an agent of socialization for children?

a. imaginary friends
b. parents
c. peer groups
d. TV

18. It's the most researched program in television history:

a. *60 Minutes*
b. *M.A.S.H.*
c. *Sesame Street*
d. *I Love Lucy*

19. According to your text, some 70 to 80 percent of all TV shows contain a degree of:

a. humor
b. violence
c. peer pressure
d. new social information

20. A study on male college students' exposure to pornography found all but which of these results?

a. heavy pornography users reported they had less confidence in females doing certain jobs
b. they tended to agree more with stereotypes of sexuality, e.g., men have greater sexual urges
c. the more pornography watched, the more its effects seemed to diminish
d. the results stood up even after rigorous statistical controls removed other potential factors

CHAPTER 22: TEST ANSWER KEYS

True/False Test

01. True	05. True	09. False	13. False
02. False	06. True	10. True	14. False
03. False	07. False	11. True	15. True
04. False	08. True	12. False	

Multiple-Choice Test

01. C	06. A	11. D	16. D
02. D	07. A	12. B	17. A
03. D	08. D	13. B	18. C
04. A	09. D	14. D	19. B
05. A	10. B	15. B	20. C

-------------- **N O T E S** --------------

Chapter 23

The Effects of Mass Communication on Behavior

Do the mass media really have an effect on us? This chapter suggests that to a degree, and for some people, the answer is "yes." As the readings suggest, these effects are usually subtle, minimal, and limited only to a few people; nevertheless, the effects *do* exist. The experiments seem to counsel the likelihood of a definite cause-and-effect relationship between media exposure and changes (good and bad) in our behavior. The long-term effects of those changes, how many of us are involved, and the degree to which media can be held liable for those changes, are things yet to be conclusively proven.

CHAPTER OBJECTIVES

. explore the new and historic concerns surrounding mass media's effects on human behavior; see what the studies suggest (but have not proven) about how people seem to react to media

. understand the difficulties involved in conducting mass media experiments, and why "proving" mass media study results is always difficult

KEY TERMS AND CONCEPTS

[ ] experiment methodology (cf. scientific method):
    [ ] survey; [ ] panel study; [ ] experiments (laboratory v. field)
[ ] opinion leaders, influence of (cf. multistep flow, Chapter 20)
[ ] 1970 National Commission on Obscenity and Pornography, results of, v. the 1986 study
[ ] prosocial behavior, definition, research results, and conceptual problems with
[ ] the "*V-chip*" technology, uses of
[ ] summary of historical trends in mass media research
[ ] catharsis theory; [ ] stimulation theory
[ ] model-rewarded v. model-punished experiment techniques
[ ] reinforcement and [ ] crystallization, media effects on political preferences
[ ] ways TV has changed the political behavior of politicians
[ ] effects of obscenity and pornography, summary effects of
[ ] television and behavioral disorders, summary effects of
[ ] future media issues: [ ] privacy; fragmentation and isolation (cocoon effect); [ ] information overload; [ ] escape

TOPICS FOR DISCUSSION

1. Your text deals with the scientific approach to the study of mass media's prosocial or antisocial effects; by comparison, what does your *common sense* or *personal experience* suggest?

2. Would you say that most political ads have a reinforcement or a crystallization effect upon you?

3. Shouldn't all laws against nonviolent pornography be banned? Why or why not?

4. If TV violence affects only a small fraction of viewers, should the majority be made to "suffer" from possible media restrictions?

5. Social, political, and personal values--like ethics--differ from person to another. If we find TV has a definite, long-term *prosocial* effect, which value system should we adopt? Who should decide? How do we adapt minority value systems to mass media distribution systems?

6. Overall, would you say that the thousands of hours you've spent in front of a TV have made your life better or worse? If you had it to watch all over again, what--if anything--would you change?

7. Do you know anyone who blames TV for an extraordinary personal or social problem?

8. Most experts believe that films (seen in theaters) are much more powerful and emotive than TV. Do you agree? Have you ever seen any unusual audience effects right after a film showing?

9. If TV violence accounts for 2-9 percent of antisocial behavior in some people, what factors do you think might account for the other 90 plus percent?

10. Name your candidates for the *Top-2 Antisocial TV Series* award; now name two candidates for the prosocial award. Compare the results with your classmates; general agreement or significant variations? How do you account for either?

11. If TV violence is bad for society--or even if it *might* be bad--why is there so much of it on TV? And why do we keep watching?

12. We humans have a poor track record as a nonviolent species. Doesn't the media simply reflect reality? Should we attempt to use the media to alter or control our fundamental nature?

13. Media research, as is obvious by now, has often centered around violence; but what about an overabundance of sitcoms, soaps, game shows, or "no brainer" programs? Can't we eventually harm ourselves as much with whip cream as with gun powder?

14. Is it even reasonable to think we can control excessive violence (or any subject) considering our First Amendment guarantees?

15. What do you believe to be the most dangerous media trend for the 21st century? Why?

Chapter 23: True/False Test

The Effects of Mass Communication on Behavior

1. Common sense, intuition, personal experience, and expert opinion are all ways to reach answers about mass media effects; what separates them from most media studies is that they don't follow scientific methodology.

2. The 1970 National Commission on Obscenity and Pornography urged that laws prohibiting the distribution of pornographic materials be repealed; a 1986 commission reversed those findings.

3. *Prosocial behavior* is conduct that's deemed socially undesirable.

4. Most media research centers on the effects of *prosocial* behavior and television violence.

5. An experimental correlation between exposure to TV violence and antisocial behavior establishes *concrete proof* of a cause-and-effect relationship between the two.

6. The *stimulation theory* of mass media effects suggests that watching TV violence may actually prompt you to act violently.

7. Media research finds little evidence to support the catharsis theory as it relates to TV violence.

8. Both boys and girls seem equally affected by TV violence.

9. In experiments where children see a peer punished for forbidden actions, most children don't seem to transfer the lesson to parallel real-life situations.

10. There is a much stronger cause-and-effect correlation between watching prosocial TV programs than antisocial TV programming.

11. Prosocial programming has come under attack from people who can't agree on what (or whose) social values to stress.

12. Recent experiments hint that TV has a dangerous and oddly strong power to convert voters from one political party to another.

13. Most political campaigns seek to keep the party faithful (the reinforcement effect) while trying to win over the undecided voters (the crystallization effect).

14. Frequent pornography consumers tend to be young, poor, poorly educated white males.

15. The Information Highway seems to promise an increase in our ability to protect personal privacy.

Chapter 23: Multiple-Choice Test

The Effects of Mass Communication on Behavior

1. Typically the longest and most expensive kind of media study is a:

    a. survey
    b. lab experiment

    c. panel study
    d. field experiment

2. Your best chance to control experimental variables is a:

    a. survey
    b. lab experiment

    c. panel study
    d. field experiment

3. Generally the only study not conducted in a "real-life" setting is a:

    a. survey
    b. lab experiment

    c. panel study
    d. field experiment

4. In the 1920s and 1930s, the public first became concerned with mass media's potential influence concerning this type of film:

    a. sex
    b. war

    c. gangster
    d. slapstick violence

5. In the 1930s some people thought radio could become a potentially dangerous medium, especially because of:

    a. false advertising
    b. excessive listener use

    c. violent programming
    d. how it was being used for political purposes

6. Since 1960, which medium seems to be singled out most often for research attention over its antisocial effects on behavior?

    a. film
    b. TV

    c. magazines
    d. music

7. Most media research focuses on how the mass media affects:

   a. adults
   b. the poor
   c. the educationally disadvantaged
   d. children and adolescents

8. Who seems most able to determine what areas of mass media get studied and how?

   a. foundations
   b. established researchers
   c. federal government
   d. university professors

9. The degree to which the antisocial effects of exposure to TV violence is complicated may be due in part to the audience's:

   a. age
   b. sex
   c. environment
   d. all the above

10. The _____ theory states that watching violence is actually healthy (since it purges desires).

    a. catharsis
    b. prosocial
    c. stimulation
    d. resonance

11. The text suggests that TV violence may account for about _____ percent of the variability in our society's collective aggressive behavior.

    a. 2-9
    b. 10-25
    c. 25-33
    d. 60-75

12. When the "undecided" voter finally makes up his or her mind for whom to vote, researchers call that the _____ effect.

    a. reinforcement
    b. crystallization
    c. resonance
    d. revelation

13. Which of these is *not* an effect of the advent of TV into the national political process?

    a. campaigns center themselves around TV exposure
    b. campaigns always include a TV consultant or advisor
    c. campaign costs have soared due to TV advertising
    d. unattractive candidates are being forced out of the process

14. When watching political ads, a party loyalist is most likely to experience the _____ effect.

    a. reinforcement
    b. crystallization

    c. resonance
    d. revelation

15. A new insight on the possible ill effects of pornography centers on differentiating the effects of:

    a. plot v. no-plot films
    b. still v. motion picture pornography

    c. violent v. nonviolent films
    d. heterosexual v. homosexual themes

16. Over the past few decades TV usage has been linked to all but which of these problems:

    a. Medicare
    b. suicides

    c. eating disorders
    d. drug and alcohol abuse

17. Research suggests that a cause-and-effect relationship exists between media violence and imitated violence only through which medium?

    a. film
    b. TV news stories

    c. TV
    d. all the above

18. One of the primary lessons to be learned from existing mass media studies is that though they may lean toward a causal relationship between some people watching TV violence and acting violently in real-life, the conclusions must be tempered with the possibility that there might be other factors operating independently of the studies' focus areas.

    a. True

    b. False

19. A "panel study" essentially surveys the same group over two or more different time periods.

    a. True

    b. False

20. One concern about the increasingly sophisticated mass media likely for the 21st century is that we will "hide ourselves away" in alternative realities. Researchers call that phenomenon the:

    a. crystallization effect
    b. V-chip effect

    c. cocoon effect
    d. none of the above

CHAPTER 23: TEST ANSWER KEYS

True/False Test

01. True	05. False	09. False	13. True
02. True	06. True	10. False	14. False
03. False	07. True	11. True	15. False
04. False	08. False	12. False	

Multiple-Choice Test

01. C	06. B	11. A	16. A
02. B	07. D	12. B	17. D
03. B	08. C	13. D	18. A
04. C	09. D	14. A	19. A
05. D	10. A	15. C	20. C

-------------- **N O T E S** --------------

TEST APPEAL PROCEDURE

1. Copies of the test will be available in Room _____ shortly after we review the test in class.

2. You may not take the test out of the room, photocopy it, or hand copy any portions of it.

3. Bring whatever documentation you might need with you to help support your appeal.

4. Do the following for *each* question you appeal:

    a. Identify the question you're appealing by number.

    b. Explain, with *convincing* and *appropriate* support, why your answer is as valid as the original answer. You may make citations from any confirmable source. If it's a source other than your text, leave it with your appeal. Make your arguments clear, complete, and concise.

    IMPORTANT: Remember that you don't have to prove my answer wrong, but rather you have to support that your answer is an acceptable one based on facts, not feelings.

    c. Fold your paper in half (lengthwise); staple multiple pages; then put your name, date, and course/section number on the top right-hand side of your paper.

    d. Put your appeal in Room _____ . It would be wise to photocopy your appeal.

5. Complete your appeal within _____ days after the test review.

6. Your appeal should be *neatly* presented.

7. I'll return your appeal, with my decision, as soon as possible.

MASS MEDIA LITERACY: A FINAL EXAM

I took the theory of this idea from E. D. Hirsch, Jr.'s book, *Cultural Literacy*. The point is that after people have reached a certain level of education (in this case, our students and this course), they ought to command a basic vocabulary of mass media terms and concepts.

Obviously this list is only a suggestion; we'll each have different ideas about which are the most important concepts in mass media, and you may want more or fewer of them. The items below come strictly from the text (most are repeated in the text glossary), so don't forget to add the ideas you bring into your course from outside sources. As a final two-hour exam, I ask students to tell me two things about each item (I usually pick fifty terms):

a. define the term accurately and concisely

b. describe the significance of each term

I weight the two items on a 40/60 split, respectively. It's also a fairly easy exam to grade; you'll be able to see right away whether they know the term (knowledge of *"b"* obviously dependent on "*a*").

I also use this list in my syllabus; in effect, I'm saying, "These ideas are the most important things I want you to take from this course; know them well." Our students may forget what *culturation analysis* is within a year, but we certainly wouldn't want them to ever forget what *prior restraint* means--or its implications. You'll notice there are certain common terms left such as CDs, VCRs, magazine, and so on; I think it would simply be a waste of space to incorporate terms and concepts that students almost surely know *before* they take this class. As I said, I've found this list concept both highly flexible and extremely useful. I hope you do too.

IMPORTANT TERMS TO KNOW

A. C. Nielsen
actual malice
advertising (and agency)
affiliates
agenda setting
AM and FM radio characteristics
Arbitron
Audit Bureau of Circulation
Authoritarian Theory
cable TV characteristics
carriage fee
circulation (controlled and paid)
commercial free speech
convergence
decoding/encoding process
demographics
Equal Opportunities Rule
ethical systems
fair use (copyright law)
Federal Communication Commission
Federal Trade Commission
First Amendment
fragmentation
Freedom of Information Act (FOIA)
gag rules
gatekeepers
hard v. soft news, characteristics
holography
injunction
Internet
invasion of privacy laws
inverted pyramid
libel (normal, *per quod*, and *per se*)
management by objectives (MBO)

modem
muckrakers
networking
news values
Nickelodeon
noise (mechanical and semantic)
opinion leaders
payola
Penny Press
pilot (TV)
polling (population and sampling issues)
pornography, problems with defining
positioning
prior restraint
public relations
rack jobbers
ratings and shares, method of determining
scientific method
shield laws
slander
socialization
Social Responsibility press theory
strategic v. tactical planning (PR)
subscription
sunshine laws
symbiotic relationships
syndicates
tabloid
telecommuting and teleconferencing
timeshifting
UHF and VHF TV, characteristics
virtual reality
wire services
yellow journalism

APPENDIX C

SUGGESTED COURSE OUTLINES

For a 10-week, 30-hour quarter or a 15-week, 30-hour semester:

#	TOPIC	CHAPTER
1	Class introductions; course overview	
2	Nature of mass media systems	1
3	Uses and functions of mass media systems	2
4	International and comparative mass media systems	3
5	History of the print media	4
6	Newspapers	5
7	Magazines	6
8	Books	7
9	History of radio and recording	8
10	Radio	9
11	Recording Industry	10
12	History of TV and film	11
13	Motion pictures	12
14-15	Television	13
16	**MIDTERM EXAM**	
17	Computers and Mass Communication	14
18	News Gathering and Reporting	15
19	Public relations	16
20	Advertising	17
21-22	Mass media laws, rules, and regulations	18
23	Ethics, codes, and media self-regulation	19
24	Audience characteristics	20
25	Feedback Systems	21
26	Mass media effects: knowledge and attitudes	22
27	Mass media effects: behavior	23
28	Selected mass media issues	
29	Final review; term paper or project reports	
30	**FINAL EXAM**	

Possible Course Outline for a 15-week, 45-hour Semester

#	TOPIC	CHAPTER
1	Class introductions; course mechanics and overview	
2	Nature of mass media systems	1
3-4	Uses and functions of mass media systems	2
5-6	International and comparative mass media systems	3
7-8	History of the print media	4
9-10	Newspapers	5
11	Magazines	6
12	Books	7
13	History of radio and recording	8
14	Radio	9
15	Sound recording	10
16-17	History of TV and film	11
18-19	Motion pictures	12
20-21	Television	13

#	TOPIC	CHAPTER
22	**MIDTERM EXAM**	

#	TOPIC	CHAPTER
23-24	Computers and Mass Communications	14
25-26	News reporting	15
27	Public relations	16
28	Advertising	17
29-30	Mass media laws, rules, and regulations	18
31-33	Ethics, codes, and media self-regulation	19
34	Audience characteristics	20
35	Feedback	21
36	Mass media effects: knowledge and attitudes	22
37	Mass media effects: behavior	23
38-41	Selected mass media issues	
42-43	In-class term paper reports and discussion	
44	Review	

#	TOPIC	CHAPTER
45	**FINAL EXAM**	

- NOTES -

- NOTES -